LOST TRAI
OF
KENT

Leslie Oppitz

COUNTRYSIDE BOOKS
NEWBURY BERKSHIRE

COUNTRYSIDE BOOKS
3 Catherine Road
Newbury, Berkshire

To view our complete range of books,
please visit us at
www.countrysidebooks.co.uk

ISBN 1 85306 996 5
EAN 978 1 85306 996 3

The cover picture shows a tram at
Maidstone's High Street terminus,
and is from an original painting by
Colin Doggett

Maps by Jennie Collins

Designed by Peter Davies, Nautilus Design

Produced through MRM Associates Ltd., Reading
Typeset by CJWT Solutions, Newton-le-Willows
Printed by Borcombe Printers plc, Romsey

CONTENTS

ACKNOWLEDGEMENTS

Acknowledgements and thanks are due to the many libraries throughout Kent who have delved into records and to John H. Meredith, Colin Withey, Derek Brice and the late J.L. Smith of Lens of Sutton for their help in the supply of many early pictures.

Grateful thanks also go to the following for help given: R.F. Appleton, Leslie Bern, Clifford Dean, Geoffrey W. Heywood, John Horne, V. Jeffery, Nicholas Kelly, David Lardge, Herbert Lingwood, Clifford N. Mewett, James Moir, Derek Redmond, Colin Smith, Hollis Motors of Dover and Peter Mann who all assisted in many ways.

Personal thanks go to Joan, my wife, without whose assistance and encouragement this might not have been written.

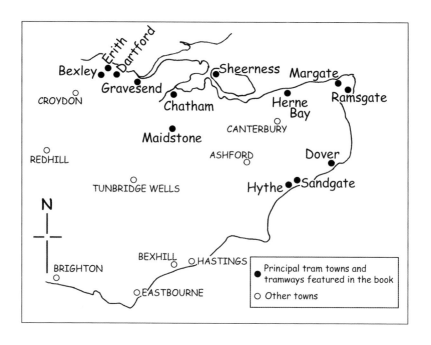

Map legend:
- Principal tram towns and tramways featured in the book
- Other towns

ABBREVIATIONS

BET	British Electric Traction Co Ltd.
BTH	British Thomson-Houston Co Ltd.
LCC	London County Council
LCDR	London, Chatham & Dover Railway
LPTB	London Passenger Transport Board
RCG&MT	Rochester, Chatham, Gravesend & Maidstone Tramways Company
SECR	South Eastern & Chatham Railway
SER	South Eastern Railway
Southmet	South Metropolitan Electric Tramways and Lighting Co Ltd.

Introduction

Surely there must be many who recall with nostalgia the electric tramway systems of Kent. Memories of the earlier days can be many and varied – from the grind of a car at full power up a hill or possibly the motion of a fast run along a reserved section of track. Others may recall the familiar clang of a gong to alert traffic in a tram's path or perhaps a time when a conductor might shout 'All Change' at a terminus and then crash the seat backs forward to face a new direction.

Trams originated in New York in 1832 where in the United States today they are still referred to as 'streetcars'. There had been great enthusiasm as two horse-drawn single-deck cars reached 'breathtaking' speeds on the flat iron strips that served as rails. In 1860 trams reached Birkenhead, introduced to this country by an American called (inappropriately) George Francis Train.

The opening of the Birkenhead system was celebrated with a banquet when all the crowned heads of Europe were invited; some 350 people were present to drink no fewer than 11 toasts. The system, just over 1¼ miles in length, opened on 30th August with the claim that it was the 'first street tramway in Europe'. The opening may have gone well but the L-shaped rails used soon caused trouble. These rails had a vertical section about 1 inch above the road and many horse-drawn carriages had their wheels ripped off when crossing at an angle. The problem was overcome by introducing grooved type rails set flush with the road surface.

London saw its first trams in March 1861 when George Train laid tracks between Marble Arch and Notting Hill Gate, with cars pulled by horses. Two other routes followed, one from Westminster to Victoria Station and another from Westminster Bridge to Kennington Park. George Train considered his tramcars a transport for the wealthy although history has shown that the reverse became true.

Although popular enough, these early ideas failed in London because L-shaped rails had been used. Lines were forced to close within a year and, as at Birkenhead, grooved-type rails were introduced

Interest in tramways developed throughout the country and many experiments followed. Trams were attempted using compressed-air systems or haulage by cable. Many cars were run by batteries with accumulators stored under the seats. But these gave off evil-smelling fumes and there was a danger that acid might spill to burn passengers' clothing. Some passengers complained that their 'seats' became hot! Tests were also carried out using oil-powered locomotives but, like their predecessors, they were not widely adopted.

It was inevitable that, with the advance of generated power, electric trams were to follow. One of the UK's earliest system was the electric tramway introduced along Brighton beach in Sussex in August 1883 and pioneered by Magnus Volk. Two years later, in September 1885, electric trams came to Blackpool. By the late 1890s many more systems were to open. On the 6th September 1897, Dover became the first town in the south of England to introduce conventional electric trams. The periodical *Railway World*, drew attention to London's continuing use of horse trams, suggesting that they should ask Dover Council for advice'.

Dover's trams were soon put to good use. In times when most people walked because money was short and horse trams were too expensive, the new transport provided a new – and cheap – method of travel where previously it had not been possible. The tram took the workman to his factory, his wife to the shops, his children to school and on Sundays made possible family trips to the park or countryside – at a price he could afford for the first time.

Further systems followed throughout the county. In 1871, a company proposed a 21-mile tramway linking Dover, Deal, Sandwich and Ramsgate but it failed through competition from the railways and, no doubt, through lack of finance. Rivalry between tram companies in earlier times was great, and it was many years before the independent Dartford, Erith and Bexley systems joined forces – and then it took a fire and the London Passenger Transport Act of 1933 to achieve it.

The story of Kent's electric tramways has its lighter moments. For instance, there is the story about the 22-stone Chatham driver who was never able to reach the top deck of his tram since he was too big to squeeze through the narrow gap at the top of the stairs. Then there is the account of the tram which was decorated when it was hired to take a newly-married couple and their guests from the church to the reception.

The Lost Tramways of Kent provides a comprehensive coverage of the lives of the county's tramways from the Bexley, Erith and Dartford systems in the west to the

Margate and Ramsgate tramways in the east. It also enables the reader to explore the very few relics that have survived in the county over the years.

Looking to the future, there could be exciting times ahead as trams in many parts of the UK make a comeback. The congested town centres in many areas today surely make it imperative for an alternative transport system to be introduced.

Leslie Oppitz

1
Metropolitan Kent

Dartford Urban District Council Tramways
Bexley Urban District Council Tramways
Erith Urban District Council Tramways
The Joyce Green Hospital Tramway, Dartford

Old Dartford High Street with car no 10 travelling eastwards towards the church, c1910. (Colin Withey collection)

Dartford Urban District Council Tramways

At about 3 am on the morning of 7th August 1917 residents in the Victoria Road area of Dartford were awakened by a fierce fire blazing in the nearby tram depot. The first person to see it was a young woman living in the house opposite, whose father ran to warn electricity station staff in the building adjoining but by this time a messenger had cycled off to fetch the fire brigade. A policeman on patrol in East Hill had also seen the blaze and had given the alarm from a High Street standard.

The local brigade were there within minutes but it was immediately obvious the fire had too great a hold and there was no hope of saving the depot or its 13 trams. The car shed was ablaze from end to end, lighting up the whole neighbourhood and covering it with a thick pall

Dartford cars photographed at the Barnham Road Depot, c 1916. The depot was completely destroyed by fire in August 1917 and never rebuilt. (Pamlin Prints)

of smoke. Soon the roof collapsed into the flames and by morning the whole of Dartford's tram fleet was nothing but a tangled mass of metal.

Despite an exhaustive enquiry, the cause was never really established. The superstitious thought it was because Dartford had 13 trams in its fleet, and others, recalling the firemen's guard of honour at the official opening 11 years earlier, saw that as an omen of the things to come. Eventually the view was accepted that a carelessly disregarded cigarette dropped by a late passenger was the probable cause.

The previous day had been August Bank Holiday and, despite the war, the public continued to enjoy their weekends and holidays. Trams offered a cheap and

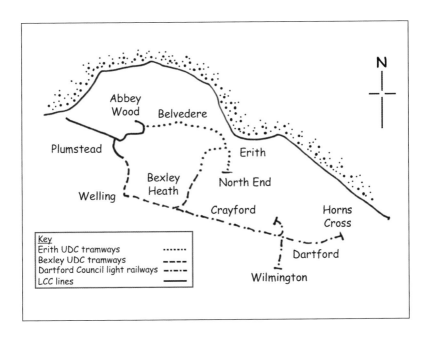

13

convenient way for both local people and travellers from south east London to spend a few hours in the countryside. This particular bank holiday had seen a considerable amount of traffic on the trams. All of the cars had been heavily worked to the point that four had broken down with overheated motors. Takings had been high and, with the cash on the premises overnight, the possibility of intruders before the fire had not been ruled out.

The immediate lack of trams caused serious problems. At that time the area, with its large munitions factories, was subject to considerable military control with transport a necessity for the munitions workers. The role of the trams was of such importance that, at 8 pm each evening, all available Dartford trams were directed to the Clock Tower at Crayford to pick up the workers from Vickers factory coming off duty.

Rescue came from neighbouring Bexley Council who, within 24 hours, provided an emergency service. Fortunately Bexley were able to hire 12 B class cars from the LCC at fairly short notice and, thanks to this, Dartford regained its full service. Initially the arrangement was for one month only but, with new cars virtually unobtainable during the war, it was subsequently agreed that Bexley Council should continue to work the Dartford lines. Bexley agreed to accept an annual rental for the use of their cars and those on hire to them.

Industry came to Dartford towards the end of the 16th century with the founding of a paper mill by Sir John Spielman, jeweller to Queen Elizabeth I. An iron rolling mill established by Geoffrey Box of Liege followed soon afterwards. As time passed, Dartford grew in industrial importance. First ideas for a horse tramway came in 1874 when powers were sought to construct a line from the Wharf at Dartford Creek, past Dartford station and via Wilmington and Farningham to Eynsford. This ambitious project was to be known as the 'Darent Valley Tramway' and its main object was to carry farm produce but, like many such early ideas, it came to nothing. It was not until 1900 that plans for an electric tramway in Dartford were proposed by a Mr Beer.

Dartford Urban District Council was not happy about this and, with other local authorities, submitted an alternative scheme. The proposal included electric trams to run from the Plumstead terminus of the Woolwich & South East London horse tramway to link Woolwich, Welling, Bexleyheath, Crayford and Dartford. Bexley Council gained its powers and commenced construction of a line from Plumstead to Bexleyheath, leaving the completion of the route eastwards in Dartford's hands. Delays followed when Dartford found that a Tramway Provisional Order could not be granted to a Rural District (Crayford was then part of Dartford Rural District) so an application had to be made under a Light Railway Order. This was, as expected, strongly opposed by the South Eastern & Chatham Railway Company (SECR), which considered tramways would prove a serious competitor, so the matter went to Parliament.

After further delays, approval was finally given on 6th February 1902. In addition a Local Act was promoted by the council giving powers to widen streets as necessary and acquire certain areas of land. In November 1902 Dartford Council made further application for an Order authorising extensions southwards to Bexley Hospital and Farningham Road station and eastwards to Craylands Lane where connection would be made with the Gravesend and Northfleet tramways already working. The latter was again strongly opposed by the SECR, which, on this occasion, was more successful. The Commissioners decided they had no powers to sanction the various lines but ultimately the Board of Trade agreed that Dartford's trams could reach Horns Cross, about 1½ miles short of the Gravesend trams.

Work on Dartford's trams began on 12th July 1905 at the Gravel Hill junction with Bexley Council Tramways, which were already operating. An order had been placed

Dartford car no 3 leads other cars at the depot to open the system on 14th February 1906. (Colin Withey collection)

with the United Electric Car Company of Preston for 12 double-deck cars mounted on Brill single trucks. These were open-top vehicles with three windows each side. The 13th car came from Erith where it had been no 15 or 16.

When completed, the lines extended from Horns Cross to Bexleyheath and from the Orange Tree at Wilmington along Lowfield Street and Hythe Street to Burnham Road where the depot was built. A ceremonial opening was held on 14th February 1906 when three cars decorated with flags and garlands toured the system. A firemen's guard of honour lined up at the depot approach, the event that was to be recalled just over 11 years later. That evening an inaugural dinner was given at the North Pole Restaurant, Hythe Street, to the staff of

A Dartford tram crosses the river Darent, c1910. Bridge House can be seen on the left. (John H. Meredith collection)

17

the contractor, J.G. White & Co Ltd, that was to work the system.

Initially the link at Gravel Hill was separated by only a few feet since Bexley Council strongly refused to allow Dartford's trams on its tracks. Eventually Bexley realised that their isolation policy was pointless and on 27th August a connection was made and Dartford cars could now reach Bexleyheath Market Place instead of having to terminate some 500 yards away.

In 1909 J.G. White & Co Ltd handed over to a firm called Balfour, Beatty & Co. Trams were now running every 20 minutes with extra journeys in the afternoons to Bexleyheath Market Place. In 1913 Dartford got its link with Gravesend but in an unwelcome form. The Gravesend and Northfleet Tramways started a motor

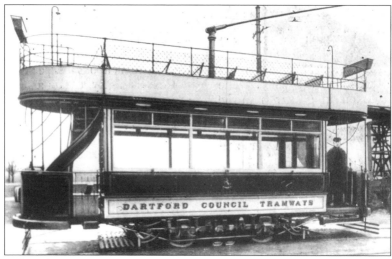

A brand new Dartford tramcar photographed in the depot yard. (Colin Withey collection)

bus service from Gravesend through Horns Cross to Dartford in direct competition with the trams. The bus service started under the fleet name of 'North Kent' but it was eventually taken over by the Maidstone and District Company.

Before electric trams came to Dartford, a horse tramway existed that was neither available to nor accessible by the public. This little tramway operated on the private roads of a group of isolation hospitals north of Dartford, today known as Joyce Green Hospital. This subject is dealt with separately at the end of this chapter.

Bexley Urban District Council Tramways

Bexley Council's Tramways Act was approved by Parliament on 26th July 1901 and authorised the construction of just over 5 route miles from Plumstead High Street through Bexleyheath to Gravel Hill with a branch line along Erith Road to the Duke of Northumberland public house at Northumberland Heath. Rather unusually, trams never reached Bexley itself, referred to locally as Old Bexley, although the power station was sited there in Bourne Road. The depot was at Gravel Hill, a solid brick building with 6 roads and a capacity for 18 cars. The council ordered 12 double-deck open-top cars from Dick, Kerr & Co, accommodating 22 passengers inside and 30 outside. They were mounted on Brush 6 ft wheelbase trucks and were fitted with electric bells and large detachable oil headlamps.

A picture taken in October 1903 on the first day of Bexley tram services en route for Plumstead. At night oil lamps were carried at the front. (Colin Withey collection)

The first six cars to arrive came by rail to Woolwich and were conveyed to the depot on a flat wagon pulled by a steam traction engine. Each came in two parts and they were finally assembled in the depot and were painted in a maroon and cream livery with the arms of Kent on the side. The remaining six cars were soon to follow. Car no 5 made the first trial run on 4th September 1903, which went satisfactorily except that grit on the rails at May Place Road gave a faulty electrical contact. Prompt action with a bucket of water remedied the situation.

There was trouble when the tramways officially

20

opened. Although the system was ceremonially opened on 1st October 1903, it could not be used by the public until two days later when the necessary Stage Carriage Licences had arrived. Then, according to local reports, the first car was deliberately obstructed by a horse bus belonging to a Mr Murray who felt he was being done out of business. The tram finally made its way by bumping the horse bus off the track!

Traffic exceeded expectations and four more cars were purchased in July 1904. Despite this, the tramway ran at a loss for the first two years. When Dartford's trams began in February 1906, as already mentioned, Bexley Council refused permission for them to reach Bexleyheath Market Place only 500 yards from the Gravel Hill terminus where tracks met end-on. Because

A Bexley car seen c1910 in its original condition. Passengers changed at Bexleyheath Market for trams to Dartford. (Colin Withey collection)

A London County Council tram found today at the East Anglia Transport Museum. Built by English Electric in 1930, it ran until the last day of London tramway operation in July 1960. (Author's collection)

of this, Dartford passengers found themselves being turned out on an open road within sight of their objective. There was much bad feeling and even a Bexley 'Electrical Engineer' wrote locally about his council's 'pettiness'. Eventually Bexley gave way and in August the lines were joined.

In 1908 Bexley UDC requested through running powers to Woolwich on LCC lines. This was granted and on 21st July of that year a trial Bexley car reached Beresford Square, Woolwich. LCC cars reached Abbey Wood 5 days later. During the First World War munitions traffic was heavy and Bexley found it necessary to hire cars from the LCC. Soon manpower shortage was affecting the system and, with the extra traffic involved, the track condition was deteriorating. Early in August 1917 the calamitous fire occurred at Dartford, and Bexley, generously forgetting the differences of the past, provided a skeleton service within 24 hours.

Erith Urban District Council Tramways

Interest in electric trams by Erith Urban District Tramways began in 1901 when the council first investigated the possibility. Erith was keen on the idea of connecting with London's tramways – even though an LCC line in Plumstead was then still being planned. Despite Erith's frequent persistence, the LCC remained disinterested and Erith's trams only ever ran on non-

Driver and conductor pose for this picture of Erith Council's tramcar no 8 waiting for departure for Abbey Wood. (Lens of Sutton)

LCC lines. It was not until London Transport days that a single track connection was made at Abbey Wood and then only to give access to Abbey Wood depot.

Erith's lines ran from Abbey Wood via Walnut Tree Road to Northumberland Heath (to face Bexley's trams end-on) and via Pier Road to North End. The bridge in Lower Road had to be built before the line could be completed and it is not difficult to imagine the reluctance with which the SECR contributed £2,500 towards its cost. Two level crossings were necessary in West Street where industrial light railways required access to riverside wharves.

Erith's tramways formally opened on 26th August 1905 with a parade of decorated cars. Fourteen double-deck four-wheel cars with Brush-built bodies had been purchased from British Westinghouse Ltd. Seven had

24

open balcony top deck covers each seating 48 passengers and the remainder had open tops seating 52 passengers. The livery was described as 'apple green and primrose'. A depot, offices and workshop were built on the west side of Walnut Tree Road close to Erith railway station. When visited by the author in February 1988 the foundations could still be traced in the overgrown wasteland but the track could not be found.

By 1906 the branch to North End was losing money and the service was reduced to workmen's cars only. Subsequently two small single-deck 'demi-cars', each seating about 20 passengers, were introduced, purchased at a total cost of £1,346. As on many buses today, the driver collected the fares as the passengers boarded the vehicle. The service began running on afternoons only in January 1907, meeting main line cars at the Wheatley Hotel. Still losses continued and eventually the service was run down to finally cease altogether by August 1909. One of the demi-cars was sold to Dartford in 1916 (to perish in the fire of 1917) and the other went to Doncaster Corporation Tramways where it became no 37.

Trouble existed between Bexley and Erith. Bexley had earlier agreed that their lines should be joined at Northumberland Heath to give Erith passengers through running to Bexleyheath Market but this did not happen until July 1908. Erith soon found the rental costs too high and terminated the service in July 1909. Through running was resumed a year later when Bexley agreed a reduction. For a while relations were friendly but in 1914 Bexley increased the rent forcing Erith, suffering losses elsewhere, to withdraw again.

Despite motorbus competition during the First World War, the need to cope with increasing traffic to the munitions factories gave Erith's trams an all-time peak in 1917. But its last profitable year was 1918–1919. From 1920 losses accumulated and the system was subsidised through the rates. Track repairs were becoming more urgent. Corrugation (an uneven track surface) was apparent in many places, resulting in complaints about noise. A priest at St Augustine's church at Belvedere claimed he had to pause each time a tram went by otherwise his words would be lost. In 1924 Erith decided to approach the LCC, saying it was prepared to lease its tramway system for a fixed period at an agreed rent. The LCC was not impressed and informed Erith it might consider an arrangement if the condition of the trams and track could be improved. Erith's trams continued to survive despite further losses and further motorbus competition. When the system passed to the London Passenger Transport Board (LPTB) in mid-1933, the council received a cash settlement and loan obligations were discharged.

The LPTB regarded the tramways of Erith, Bexley and Dartford as a single operating unit. With greater flexibility, cars could be transferred to meet requirements in the various localities. Twelve covered-top M class cars were soon to arrive at Bexleyheath depot and a similar number of Bexley open-topped cars were removed to Abbey Wood for storage. More changes followed with improvements to the fleet, and where titles such as 'Erith Council Tramways' appeared on cars, these were painted out and suffix letters (Erith was 'D') substituted. At Erith at least the coat of arms remained.

Bexley and Erith cars meet at Northumberland Heath. The last tram at Bexley ran on 23rd November 1935. (Colin Withey collection)

After two years of operation the LPTB had considerably improved tram services in the area. The Wilmington branch south of Dartford had gone because of the poor quality single track and duplication by buses. Even so, it was the Board's declaration that trams would be replaced by trolleybuses and, to this end, the necessary wide-sweeping powers were obtained in July 1934. Work was put in hand on the south east London routes in 1935 and the Board decided that the Bexleyheath and Erith tram depots were not suitable for trolleybus conversion. A trolleybus depot – London Transport's first – was purpose-built in Erith Road near its junction with May Place Road, headquarters of today's 'Bexleybus' system.

Car no 9 at the Wheatley Hotel, Erith. The hotel was demolished in the early 1980s to make way for a roundabout. (John H. Meredith collection)

When visited in 2005, Erith's tram depot, offices and workshop had been completely demolished. This picture was taken after closure of the depot. (Lens of Sutton)

The last tram between Abbey Wood and Bexleyheath via Erith ran on the night of 9th November 1935 and trolleybuses on route 698 began the next morning running from Woolwich Free Ferry to a turning point at Bexleyheath round the small triangle of streets at the Clock Tower. The conversion of the Woolwich-Bexleyheath-Dartford section followed when the last trams ran shortly before midnight on 23rd November 1935. The depot at Erith was demolished as recently as the early 1980s along with the nearby Wheatley Hotel where the area is now a roundabout. The Bexleyheath tram depot off the Broadway was demolished to make way for civic offices whereas the trolleybus depot in Erith Road became a bus depot.

Some 30 years of trams around Dartford, Erith and Bexleyheath had come to an end.

The Joyce Green Hospital Tramway, Dartford

In the latter part of the 19th century, local government in London was concerned about fever and smallpox cases among the poor and in 1870/1 opened hospitals in Hampstead, Stockwell and Homerton. These were available just in time for a serious smallpox epidemic, during which time some 16,000 cases were admitted. There were soon complaints about such hospitals in built-up areas and a Royal Commission appointed to investigate recommended that smallpox should be treated in isolated situations on the banks of the Thames or in floating hospitals on the river itself. In 1881 two old wooden battleships, the *Atlas* and the *Endymion* anchored off Greenwich, were acquired and in 1884 they were removed to new moorings at Long Reach off Dartford Marshes.

In 1893 the Board decided that, with the risk of fire or collision always possible in a busy stretch of waterway, the ships should be replaced by a permanent smallpox hospital on shore. Plans were put in hand for a large hospital to be built on an adjacent parcel of land near Joyce Green Farm but there were delays in obtaining a loan and construction did not commence until 1899. However, because of a brief outbreak of smallpox in 1895 it was decided to go ahead with construction of a horse tramway along a causeway from Long Reach Pier to the

Horse trams at Joyce Green Hospital in the mid-1920s. The tramway was built to convey smallpox patients from river steamers to the hospitals. (Picture courtesy of Dr John Burne, Hon Archivist, Joyce Green Hospital)

new hospital area. This was to ensure that patients had a smooth journey after arriving by river steamer.

The contract for the roads and tramways went to Mr J. Dickson of St Albans who sub-contracted some of the tramway work to Dick, Kerr & Co. The tramway, comprising a single line of 4 ft gauge with passing places, was completed by May 1897. In the winter of 1901/2 there were 7,000 reported cases of smallpox and a temporary 300-bed hutted hospital was quickly

When horse trams were able to reach the hospital's entrances. The arches have since been removed. (Picture courtesy of Dr John Burne, Hon Archivist, Joyce Green Hospital)

constructed at Long Reach, opening on 27th February 1902. At first patients were conveyed in horse-drawn ambulances but the Board also purchased two second-hand horse tramcars from the Harrow Road & Paddington Tramway Co for £45 each, putting them in service after altering their gauge.

In April 1902 the Board purchased without prior inspection four more cars, two from Burnley and two from Huddersfield. On arrival these were found to be heavy steam tramway trailers and quite unsuitable. By 1904 their bogies had been sold for scrap and the bodies were placed in the grounds to serve as shelters for convalescent patients! Two further tramcars bought subsequently proved more successful.

A second and larger hospital was erected at the Orchard and connected with the tramway. On 28th December 1903 a permanent smallpox hospital at Joyce Green with 938 beds was formally opened and the hospital ships sold by auction. A 'coach house' and stables were provided in a walled enclosure. The tramway increased to its maximum extent of almost 3½ miles and further cars were purchased including four ambulance vehicles.

Electric traction was never introduced, probably because of lack of supply – the hospital was lit by gas until 1925. In 1912 there was a proposal to fit trams with petrol engines but this was dropped in favour of separate petrol locomotives, possibly to avoid vibration in the cars. In July 1914 a motor tractor was tested hauling two trams laden with 23 adults and this proved successful but with war soon to follow the idea was abandoned, since no motor vehicles could be spared.

Motor traction was not considered again until 1924/5. Tests with a Talbot motor ambulance proved successful and two more were ordered. Speeds were kept low but motors, unlike horses, could not exert the same sideways pull at curves and tram brakes-men were obliged to alight and lean against the side of the car to help it round! From 1930, with road ambulances available, the tramway remained solely as an internal link between the hospitals. According to records, the cars were last used in 1936. The cars were dismantled in 1938 and the track lifted in 1943 as part of a wartime drive for scrap metal.

Long Reach Hospital was demolished in the early 1970s in connection with development for the Thames Flood Barrier, and the wooden huts of Orchard Hospital had been previously destroyed by incendiary bombs in 1940. Beforehand they had been used to accommodate refugees from Dunkirk and serve as a temporary base for troops. When the author visited the area some years ago, the course of the tramways was still clearly visible along the causeway and in the hospital grounds. The transport office was once the tack room and marks on the wall's wooden panelling showed where horses' tackle had been kept. Next door the stables were just as they had been and a wooden chute remained which had fed the horses with hay and oats from an overhead store. Outside, the tracks leading to the car shed were still in position.

But today Joyce Green Hospital no longer exists and its buildings have been demolished. The land has become part of the Thames Gateway Development Area and the hospital facilities have been transferred to Darenth Valley Hospital.

2

A Pioneer Among Electric Trams

Gravesend & Northfleet Electric Tramways Ltd

A Gravesend double-deck tram, c1910. Regular electric tram services began in Gravesend in 1902 to last 27 years. (Photograph courtesy of Gravesend Central Library)

The first trams in Gravesend were built by the Gravesend, Rosherville and Northfleet Tramway Company under an Act of 1881. The trams were horse-drawn, the gauge was 3 ft 6 ins and a modest service operated from Gravesend High Street to the Leather Bottel in Northfleet. Only five cars were available, all single-deck, each seating 22 people and pulled by one horse.

The horses were hired from a Mr G.W. Brooks, a farmer at Chalk, who arranged that the horses that pulled dustcarts for the council during the week were available to pull trams on Saturdays. In addition, the animals were available for fire duty and, if an alarm was raised, it was not unusual for the fire engine to 'borrow' its horse from any passing tram with the passengers being left stranded until the fire was out!

In 1884 application was made to extend the line from the Leather Bottel to Huggins College, near Northfleet station. The request, refused in 1881, was approved on this occasion but trams elsewhere were not proving very successful and the company did not undertake the work. Huggins College, an almshouse for 'impoverished

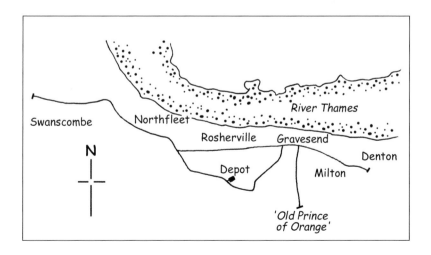

tradesmen', was demolished in 1968. It was replaced by a block of flats although the gates remained standing.

When a Huggins College tramway extension was eventually built, it was undertaken by the Series Electric Traction Company, which was interested in trying out a new type of electric tramway operation. A gauge of 3 ft 6 ins was agreed and the new concern pointed out to the horse tram company that the line could be equally worked by horses. Two electric trams were supplied by the Falcon Engineering Co of Loughborough (predecessors of Brush Electrical Engineering Co) and powered by Ewell Parker traction motors.

The system used a positive and negative cable built into an underground conduit. Each car carried a long skate collector consisting of bronze strips, insulated from each other, running inside the conduit to collect and return the current. The collector was connected to the car by bars, which passed through a slot immediately inside one running rail. At regular intervals in the conduit the supply cable was broken by a pair of plates held together by springs. The collector was fitted with chisel points at each end and, on contact, the plates were separated and connection was maintained with the motor of the car until the collector passed on to the next pair of plates.

In this way any number of cars could use the line at the same time in series with each other. Current came from a generator capable of producing 30,000 watts and the consumption for one car was 60 amps at 165 volts. The speed, limited by the Board of Trade to 6 miles per hour, was controlled by a switch on the car. By reversing the current a car could stop within its own length. The *Illustrated London News* of 6th April 1889 described the

'Series' system as 'the first electric tram-line in Europe with every indication of great success'.

Experiments were carried on for about 18 months. There are reports that the line opened to the public on 16th April 1889 but other accounts do not support this, suggesting that trial runs were made with numbers of schoolchildren only. Whatever the truth of the matter, the electric trams had gone by November 1890 with the company pulling out to attempt different experiments elsewhere. After the equipment had been removed, the line appears to have reverted to horse cars once again covering the whole route from Huggins College to the Clock Tower.

In 1895 the local council complained that the half-hourly service provided by the small one-horse cars was quite inadequate for the area. Three years later, under continued pressure, four of the single-deckers were replaced by double-decker cars each requiring two horses. Two of these were the 'knifeboard' type with the upper deck seats back-to-back. These gave some improvement with cars of greater capacity able to provide a 20 minute service at busy times but it was still not enough.

Further thoughts of electric trams came in 1899 when a controlling interest in the company was obtained by the Drake and Gorham Electric Power and Traction Syndicate Ltd (later renamed 'The National Electric Traction Company Limited'). A Bill was promoted to reconstruct the existing route to standard gauge and include additional lines through Gravesend and to Denton. The object was to electrify throughout and provide a link to Dartford and London. However, legal negotiations became protracted and no work was done. On 1st January 1901 the undertaking was resold to the British Electric Traction Company group (BET) for £21,064.

The BET's first action was to call the company the 'Gravesend and Northfleet Electric Tramways Limited'. The new company was registered on 18th April 1901 when all horse tram operations ceased. Hopes had remained that trams could still link with a system planned at Dartford (it opened later in 1906) through to London. Had that happened, then through services might have been available from east of Gravesend across London to the far side of the capital! Not unexpectedly the move was bitterly opposed by the South Eastern & Chatham Railway (SECR) whose line it would have paralleled. The 1½ mile link that could have come between the Gravesend trams at Swanscombe and Dartford's trams at Horns Cross was never joined.

The new tramway company removed the narrow-gauge tracks converting them to 4 ft 8½ in standard gauge and ordered 20 double-deck cars from Dick, Kerr and Co. On arrival the trams were parked in sidings at Rosherville station from where they were towed the 100 yards to the tram track near the Dover Road depot. The first line opened on 2nd August 1902, providing a service from the Leather Bottel to the Clock Tower. By 22nd September extensions had opened to Denton, Swanscombe and Pelham Road. The Dover Road section was opened on 30th January 1903 and the final section along Windmill Street to the Old Prince of Orange did not open until 4th December 1903.

Gravesend car no 18 at the Clock Tower en route to Denton, c. 1906. Regular electric tram services commenced in August 1902 to last 27 years. (Lens of Sutton)

Of the 20 open-top cars ordered, ten were four-wheelers and the other ten mounted on bogies. It was soon apparent that the bogie cars were too large for the system and also put too heavy a strain on the local electricity works particularly when climbing hills such as those at Stonebridge in Northfleet. These were sold over a period from January 1904 with two going eventually to Jarrow, four to Swansea and the remaining four to South Metropolitan Electric Tramways (Southmet) of Croydon in February 1906.

Traffic on the Windmill Street and Dover Road routes soon proved disappointing and, to cut running costs, two small one-man operated cars were built and supplied to Gravesend in April 1904. The single-deck

These single-deck cars in Gravesend, which seated 16 in the saloon and 6 more in the end vestibules, proved highly successful on certain hilly routes. (Photograph courtesy of Gravesend Central Library)

cars seated 16 in the saloon and 6 more in the end vestibules and were fitted with a newly-patented system of regenerative control. This control included an effective braking system, which was considered necessary after recent accidents in neighbouring hilly areas. In addition it was claimed that the regenerative system 'pumped current back into the overhead wires when braking thus reducing operating costs'. In tests carried out, the 'demi-cars' proved successful. They could be perfectly controlled on a gradient of 1 in 11 and further such sets were ordered.

To replace the ten cars sold, four Brush open-top four-wheelers were obtained in 1905 (source unknown) and

Gravesend's open-topped car no 7 photographed in Pelham Road. Until 1921 the livery of the cars was maroon and cream with the BET 'magnet and wheel' painted in blue and silver. (Picture courtesy of Gravesend Central Library)

two similar but slightly smaller cars came from Jarrow in 1908. It was not until 1921 that two further cars were purchased from Taunton, these being single-deck cars each seating 24 passengers.

Gravesend's trams had wooden seats and, until 1921, the livery was of maroon and cream. The usual BET 'magnet and wheel' badge appeared in the centre of the waist panel painted in blue and silver. Commercial advertising began at an early date. In the book *Tramways of Kent,* edited by the late G.E. Baddeley, it is reported that a coal merchant made an offer in July 1904 by advertising on the back of tram tickets. He promised that he would give 2 tons of coal free to the

Before the days of the popular motor car. A Denton tram waits in a loop in Gravesend's New Road c. 1905. (Lens of Sutton)

passenger who sent him the largest number of used tickets by 31st December. Whether he did or not is not known but the BET was not happy with this form of advertising and took it up with the Gravesend Company because children were pestering alighting passengers for their tickets.

Often individual tramcars carried exclusive advertisements, such as car no 1 which was used by Russell's Brewery of Gravesend for their 'Shrimp Brand Beer' for a period just before the First World War. The car was painted white all over with a shrimp figuring large on the dash while the advertiser's name and other slogans adorned every other possible place. Inside the car were photographs of the various public houses owned by the company. Nobody boarding the car could be left in any doubt as to what beer they should drink!

A Denton-Swanscombe tram passes along King Street while a Raworth Patent 'demi-car' no 10 waits in Windmill Street c. 1906. (Lens of Sutton)

The war brought much new industry to the area, which placed a heavy burden on the tramways. From 1915 onwards the Windmill Street service reverted to double-deck operation with the demi-cars being used on the Dover Road section where traffic was still light. In addition to the usual blackout precautions, the destination boxes were removed. The cars suffered badly from the difficulty of obtaining spare parts and the paintwork began to deteriorate. On certain cars bolts were driven into the top plates of the controllers so the handles could not be turned beyond the fourth notch thus reducing the speed and preventing further wear. After the war in 1920 there was much adverse criticism locally that claimed the trams were 'completely unsafe and unroadworthy'. The newly-formed Ministry of

Transport was called in and after a full investigation the system was reported to be quite safe to continue in operation. But the trams were now losing money and an offer by the company to withdraw them completely was refused by the council who pointed out that if the company closed then all equipment would have to be removed and all rails lifted.

During the life of the trams, there were a number of isolated incidents. There had been one fatal accident in 1903 when a man was killed by a tram and in 1920 an elderly lady fell under a tram in King Street during heavy traffic and died later in hospital. In 1922 there was a lucky escape when railings at Rosherville saved a car from falling 70 feet into a quarry after it had jumped the points and mounted the pavement.

In 1921 the tramway company set about improving its standards. The track from St James's church (demolished in 1966/7) to the Leather Bottel was relaid and the cars were given a new livery of red and cream. New equipment was fitted and a number of cars were fitted with covered tops. Trams appeared in hospital carnivals to help raise money for Gravesend Hospital. For a time it seemed the critics had been silenced but it remained a losing battle. Many of the routes were proving unprofitable but any closure was still refused by the local council.

In the late 1920s, in the face of increasing competition from buses, and as an economy measure, inspectors were abolished. The tramways declined still further and eventually the company was able to reach an agreement with the local councils and the Maidstone & District bus company by securing an Amendment Order in 1928, which allowed buses to take the place of trams. In this way control of the tramways was passed officially to the Maidstone & District Motor Services Ltd at the beginning of 1929 thus making the Gravesend system the first electric tramway in the Greater London area to close completely.

The final tram ran on 28th February 1929 after which time the car bodies were sold off at the depot at £10 for a covered-top car and £5 for an open-top car. No 1, once the pride of the fleet, was soon to be seen in its bright red and cream livery in a garden near the depot whereas no 14, newly painted only a few months previously, seemed somewhat incongruous (and rather sad) in another garden in the Perry Street district. No 13 had stood

A conductor reverses the trolley pole on Gravesend car no 3 ready for a return journey. When the system closed in 1929, car bodies were sold off at £10 or £5 each. (Picture courtesy of Gravesend Central Library)

outside the depot with its number blacked out in case any prospective purchaser might be superstitious.

The building that was once a tram depot can still be found today partly modified and existing as a local factory behind the Bridge Inn in the Dover Road at Northfleet. From time to time when roads are dug up or widened, sections of tram track have been excavated. Near the Old Prince of Orange in Windmill Street sections of track still exist below the surface. Some years ago a Gravesend tram body was found at Allhallows but it was beyond restoration. But the upper railings live on, fitted to Lowestoft 14 at the East Anglia Transport Museum at Carlton Colville.

3
One of Britain's Smallest Tramway Systems

The Sheerness & District Electrical Power and Traction Co Ltd

Sheerness car no 7 when new at the depot. Regular electric tram services began at Sheerness in April 1903. (Colin Withey collection)

Why trams ever came to Sheerness remains a mystery. When a Light Railway Order was initially approved it covered a mere 2½ miles of route with little opportunity to expand. Twelve cars were supplied but four of these were later despatched elsewhere being surplus to requirements.

In 1900 the British Electric Traction (BET) group financed an electric generating station on the Isle of Sheppey. This was a Kingsway, London company, which also became involved in tramway systems at Gravesend and Croydon and even as far afield as Wellington, New Zealand. BET established a subsidiary company calling it the 'County of Kent Electrical Power Distribution Company Ltd' on 24th April 1900 with a capital of £25,000. It was agreed this company should provide Sheerness with a tramway system and an application for a Light Railway Order was filed the following month. Powers were asked for a line from

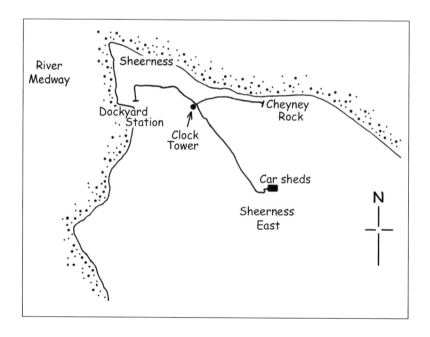

Sheerness Pier via the Clock Tower to Sheerness East station and Halfway House with a branch from the Clock Tower to Cheyney Rock. In addition branches were sought from Halfway House to Queenborough station and to Minster.

When authorisation was granted on 12th February 1901, only tram routes north of Sheerness East station were agreed. The Sheppey Light Railway Company, already building a railway from Queenborough to Leysdown, virtually cutting the tramway system in half, felt strongly that trams would compete with their traffic. Consequently the railway company's objection to the prospect of tramlines crossing their tracks was upheld and Sheerness's trams, restricted to 2½ miles of track, were almost doomed before they began.

Contractors to build the tramway system were J.G. White & Co Ltd with track laid to a gauge of 3 ft 6 ins. Permission from the railway company had to be obtained before laying tracks in front of Sheerness Town station where there was heavy cab traffic. After discussion, it was agreed tracks could be laid against the north kerb with a loop in the centre of the road thus leaving cab traffic free at the station entrance.

The generating station was built at Sheerness East adjacent to the railway station. The manager was Mr Cutbush, who was also mainly responsible for the design. Mr Cutbush was very proud that the steel chimney was the first to be erected in the district. The dynamos were driven by power from diesel engines (supplied from a Swiss firm); these were also the first of this type in Sheppey. The station included a large battery room for use in emergencies or on very light loads.

Children pose by trams at Sheerness Clock Tower, c1910. Cars are about to depart for Halfway House and the Dockyard respectively. (Colin Withey collection)

The Clock Tower at Sheerness photographed in 2005. Sheerness claimed to have one of Britain's smallest tramway systems. (Derek Brice)

The open-top trams were built and equipped by Brush Electrical Engineering Co Ltd of Loughborough and seated 22 inside and 28 outside. They looked resplendent in two shades of chocolate brown with gold-lined panels and lettered 'Sheerness Tramways' on their sides. They were brought into Sheppey by train and unloaded at Sheerness East station – all 12 of them! The drivers wore chocolate brown uniforms to match and the inspectors wore black with gold braid.

The trams were unique since they used Siemen's bow collectors instead of the usual trolley wheel to pick up the current from the overhead wires. Unique because no other Siemen's bows were used on British double-deck cars and the only other open-top cars to use such collectors were in Tasmania – and even these soon received roof covers.

Trams in Bridge Street cross The Moat. Sheerness' trams were unique being equipped to draw current through large overhead Siemens bow collectors. No other British tramways used this method. (Lens of Sutton)

The bow was fixed to a tubular stanchion positioned in the centre of the top deck and stood about 5 ft high. The two arms holding the bow were fixed to the crown of the stanchion and running parallel extending to a distance of 10 ft or so from the back of the tram. As the arms neared the end they opened out to take the bow, which was about 4 ft in length. It was made of aluminium in which there was a deep groove. This was filled with a kind of vaseline and, upon any sudden application of power, a shower of flaming sparks descended. During their use on the trams the bows were gradually shortened until there was no overhang at all.

During construction of the tramway system, roads were 'in a chaotic mess for quite a while'. Another problem soon arose. With the exception of a section of track near the railway station, which had stone setts (rectangular paving blocks), the roads were of macadam. Consequently the traffic, especially in wet weather when wheels skidded across the lines, tended to scoop out the macadam leaving the rails well above road level. Eventually granite blocks were placed alongside the rails and the position was eased.

According to the *Sheerness Times*, the first car ran at 8.12 am from the Clock Tower on 9th April 1903 during the Easter holidays when the public scrambled for seats on the new system. The opening was followed by a 12 minute interval service on both routes – to Cheyney Rock and Sheerness East – from 8 am to 10.30 pm. Special workmen's cars were available from 6.40 am. It was soon apparent, however, that the service was more than sufficient and the main route was reduced to 15 minute intervals. On the Cheyney Rock route normal

Trams in Sheerness commenced in April 1903 and lasted only 14 years. With the railway company refusing to allow trams south of Sheerness East Station, the system was doomed almost before it began. (Lens of Sutton)

services were stopped apart from workmen's cars. It became equally apparent that, with no prospect of reaching Queenborough and Minster, 12 cars were too many. Within a few months four cars were sold to the City of Birmingham Tramways Co within the BET group and the Sheerness fleet was reduced to eight.

Two weeks from opening there was an accident. It happened in Meyrick Road when a bow collector fractured, falling to the ground and injuring three people. In the following year on 1st May a car left the track and struck a building at 220, High Street. Despite the various problems, a profit of £78 was made in the first year even though a claim was made by a local councillor that the trams were the noisiest in England!

With traffic remaining light on the Cheyney Rock route, the company applied during 1904 for powers to run one-man 'demi-cars'. In addition an existing car was modified with the stairs blocked off and entrance only by the front off-side. No doubt at the time with little road traffic this did not cause a traffic hazard but passengers did complain they had lost their sea view from the upper deck.

In 1910, seven years after the trams had commenced, the company made another attempt to expand its routes. This time proposals were put forward for a line from Sheerness East to Minster parallel with the railway line and without the need to cross it. A public enquiry was held at Tower's Hall (later Nokes' Garage) when proposals were put forward but the idea was strongly opposed by Lord Jersey and others of the Light Railway Committee – and they won their case. The tramway

A tram passes the Conservative Club in Broadway on the Cheyne Rock route c. 1910. The Clock Tower can be seen in the distance. (Lens of Sutton)

company had to remain content with its mere 2½ miles of track. With expansion denied, the end of the tramway system was inevitable.

Buses commenced in 1913 when a firm named T. Standen & Sons from Sittingbourne began a service with two double-deck vehicles. Freed from earlier restrictions imposed by the railway, the buses cut deeply into the tram company's meagre traffic.

The war delayed closure but on 14th June 1917 BET told the Sheerness Urban and Rural District Councils that the Sheerness Tramways would cease operation unless the councils were willing to buy the sections in their relevant areas. This both councils declined since they considered the tramway system insolvent. The line ended quietly on Saturday, 7th July 1917 without ceremony. It had lasted only 14 years and had the distinction of being the first regular electric tramway system in the British Isles to close down.

According to the *Sheerness Times-Guardian*, it was not long before 'hordes of men descended on the town pulling up rails, dismantling wires and heaving out posts'. The whole lot was carted off to the Town station for despatch since 'the country needed the steel for the war effort'. But there much of it stayed until the war was over!

In 1918 the remaining tramcars were sold to the Darlington Corporation and some of the point-works were sold to Chatham for further use. Today there is virtually nothing left for the historian to find. Even the level crossing at Sheerness East station, which once barred the tramway's progress, had gone by 1950 when the Queenborough–Leysdown branch was axed by British Rail.

4
Trams Around a Dockyard

Chatham & District Light Railways Co and Rochester Corporation Tramways

An open-topped tram bound for Chatham Cemetery. Because of the narrow roads along the route the gauge for Chatham's tracks was 3 ft 6 ins. (Colin Withey collection)

On 30th October 1902 four people were killed and 54 injured in a serious accident at the bottom of Westcourt Street in Old Brompton, north of Chatham, when an electric tram went out of control. It was 6.40 am when tramcar no 19, laden with more than 60 dockyard

Brush car no. 32 complete with new coloured route letter board heads a line of trams waiting at Chatham Dockyard gates in 1903. (Lens of Sutton)

workers, was the first to descend Westcourt Street that morning. Due to the steep gradient of 1 in 9½, all cars were required to stop at the top of the hill and again at the foot before taking the points into Dock Road. A speed limit of 4 mph had been imposed and as a further safeguard inspectors acted as 'pilots' to cars descending.

According to the *Chatham Observer*, it had been raining on the morning in question and the track was obviously greasy. Car no 19 stopped at the top of the hill as required and waited for the pilot. After four minutes the pilot appeared at the bottom of the hill but the driver, who no doubt carried many impatient passengers, set the car in motion rather than wait for him. The car gained speed rapidly and was soon out of control. At the bottom the tram could not negotiate the curve, with the result that the vehicle overturned onto its right side.

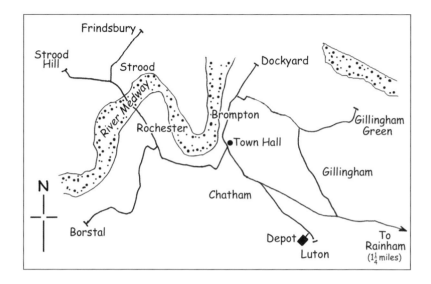

The tram was wrecked and many of the passengers on the outside were thrown with some force onto the pavement. Inside the car the passengers were 'thrown into a heap and badly cut by the shattered glass'. Almost as if to emphasise the danger of the steep hill a further car, fortunately without any passengers, got out of control later the same day while workmen were still clearing the wreckage of the first accident. Happily the tram remained on the track and was brought to a standstill after negotiating the corner.

At a subsequent inquiry it was agreed that the high number of deaths and injuries was due not only to the driver's lack of skill but also to the conductor's failure to enforce regulations. It transpired he had allowed 32 people on the open top (there were only 28 seats) and a further 29 passengers inside where there were 24 seats.

In addition the inquiry discovered that the pilot had not cleaned and sanded the rails that morning before the service had begun.

The findings stipulated that an alternative route should be found immediately with the consequence that a parallel street known as Middle Street was subsequently used, having a slightly less difficult gradient. Even so a warning speed restriction, coloured red, was displayed on a tram standard to remain there throughout the life of the trams.

Tramways first came to the Medway towns in 1902. Towards the end of the 19th century there had been horse buses but the area had been too hilly for horse trams with many roads long and steep. Trams were initially considered as far back as 1893 but these ideas came to nothing. It was not until October 1897 that the Rochester, Chatham, Gillingham & District Electric Railways Co Ltd registered in accordance with the provisions of the Light Railway Act of the previous year.

In November 1897 the company applied to the Board of Trade for an Order to build some 14 miles of track of 4 ft 8½ in gauge for electric trams covering the Rochester and Chatham areas. The commissioners agreed in principle but with many roads so narrow it was recommended that the gauge should be reduced to 3 ft 6 ins. In addition all the Rochester lines were dropped due to the town's opposition to trams. The revised scheme was adopted on 6th June 1898 and a Light Railway Order was granted on 17th August 1899. At the same time a new company with a less cumbersome title was incorporated, the Chatham & District Light Railways

Company, a subsidiary of the British Thomson-Houston Company.

A powerhouse and depot were built on three acres of land at Luton not far from the Hen and Chickens public house. The depot was quite large for the system, having accommodation for 60 cars on eight roads all under cover – more than would ever be needed. Construction work elsewhere took over two years to complete. An overhead wire system was adopted with the wires suspended from single poles with bracket arms. The track was laid on a concrete foundation and this fact, plus the quality of the rails supplied by the Haematite Steel Co, made very smooth riding possible throughout the tramway system's life.

Initial stock consisted of 25 open-topped four-wheeled cars supplied during April and May 1902 by George F. Milnes & Co. They were painted light grass green and ivory with the title 'Chatham & District Light Railways' appearing in gold shaded letters on the rocker panel. The trucks and bodies were delivered separately at Chatham railway sidings and taken by road to the depot where they were assembled. The cars were built to accommodate 24 passengers inside and 28 on top. They were each fitted with two British Thomson-Houston motors of 25 hp each and equipped with hand and mechanical track brakes. After the Old Brompton accident, Westinghouse magnetic track brakes were fitted to all cars.

Trial running began in May 1902 and before long the public were getting used to the idea of seeing trams throughout the district run for driver training. Prospective passengers did not have to wait long for

Members of the Omnibus Society turn out to inspect the ex-Maidstone car no 52 at Luton Depot in August 1930. (Lens of Sutton)

their new transport for at noon on Tuesday, 17th June 1902, the system was officially opened. It was a ceremonial affair before a number of local dignitaries, including the Mayor of Chatham. Afterwards a special luncheon was held in Chatham Town Hall.

A full public service began the next day covering routes from Luton via Chatham Town Hall to the Dockyard, Chatham Cemetery via Brompton and Gillingham to Victoria Bridge, Chatham Town Hall via Jezreels Corner to the 'White House' in Pier Road and Chatham (ex-LCDR) station to the Docks. Trams ran every 15 minutes except the last route, which was half-hourly. A service to Gillingham Green began by extending the Cemetery–Victoria Bridge route soon after the opening.

A car bound for Rainham passes Chatham Town Hall, probably in the late 1920s. (Lens of Sutton)

In the same year an ambitious proposal was made by the Rochester, Chatham, Gravesend & Maidstone Tramways Co to construct a tramway system, alternatively to utilise vehicles 'worked by electricity on the overhead trolley system and not running on fixed rails' – better described as trolleybuses! Lines to Maidstone and Gravesend were proposed plus running powers over Chatham's lines. Not surprisingly this upset the Chatham & District Company which countered with its own Bill to extend further in Chatham, construct new lines in Rochester and build 'interurban' lines to Maidstone, Gravesend and Rainham.

At this stage Rochester became involved. Having earlier rejected trams, it now saw Chatham's system proving successful and wanted some of its own. Since Chatham and Rochester were in effect one connected

Trams pass Chatham Town Hall, c1910. Electric trams began in Chatham in June 1902 and lasted 28 years. (Colin Withey collection)

Chatham's Town Hall building in 2005. (Derek Brice)

A Chatham tram crosses Medway Bridge, c1910. When powers were sought to cross the Medway to reach Strood there was bitter opposition from the South East & Chatham Railway but agreement was given and services commenced from 1908. (Photograph W.E. Crawforth/John H. Meredith collection)

town, the idea seemed an absurdity and was typical of the many rivalries and incongruities between so many areas in all parts of the country. Despite this, Rochester submitted a Bill in November 1902 seeking powers to build over five miles of track.

With three Bills now before Parliament, there was much arguing between the companies concerned. As support mustered for the Chatham & District Company, the concern proposing trams or 'trolleybuses' to Maidstone and Gravesend dropped out. This left Chatham and Rochester who eventually got together and reached a compromise solution. It was agreed that

Medway Bridge, 2005. In 1911 the bridge was rebuilt taking more than three years but tram services to Strood Hill and Frindsbury were maintained on temporary track. (Derek Brice)

Rochester could share Chatham's power station and in return Rochester agreed to build its own lines and lease them to the Chatham company.

The Bill received Royal Assent on 11th August 1903 and the tramways extended into Rochester between the years 1904 and 1908 – despite bitter opposition from the South Eastern & Chatham Railway (SECR). The town maintained some of its independence by incorporating the city's coat of arms on the pole bases. By December 1904, Chatham's Gillingham Green service was able to extend beyond Chatham Town Hall down Rochester's Star Hill and by May 1908 trams were crossing the river

Medway to reach the top of the long and dangerous Strood Hill and along Frindsbury Road as far as Bingham Road.

On the latter route, trams along Frindsbury Road passed over a railway tunnel used by trains between Strood and Higham. When completed in 1824, this tunnel had been part of the Thames and Medway Canal allowing barges to reach Chatham from the river Thames with the intention of saving a 47 mile passage around the Isle of Grain. When the canal failed in 1844 through competition from the railway, the canal owners sold out to the railway company and soon a single track was built through the tunnel over the canal! The situation did not last and in 1846 the SER took over whereupon the canal was filled in and double track was laid. Today's railway passengers may notice a flash of daylight as they pass halfway through the tunnel – this was a section cut out where barges passed each other over 160 years ago.

A further ten cars had been delivered in 1903 with the bodies built by Brush Electrical Engineering Co Ltd of Loughborough. They appeared smaller, having three main windows each side instead of four as in the earlier cars. Also in 1903 car no 36 was delivered, this being similar in appearance to the earlier cars. It is thought this was a replacement to the ill-fated no 19 and had to be built similarly for insurance purposes.

Meanwhile extensions to the tramway system continued. Priestfields was reached in May 1906 but perhaps the most ambitious was the opening of a route to Rainham opened in August 1906 where much of the track had been laid in the fields alongside Watling Street, the main road to Dover. There were serious intentions at the time to extend the route to join the narrow-gauge system at Maidstone but the plans, although agreed, were never pursued. In 1907 ten more Brush cars (reverting to four side windows) were delivered to cope with increased business and by 1908 the Priestfields route was extended to reach Borstal.

In 1911 two more Brush cars were purchased plus three United Electric cars. In the same year work commenced to rebuild Rochester Bridge, an operation that was to take more than three years. During this time it was possible to maintain tram services to Strood Hill and Frindsbury at first by a double track on a wooden temporary bridge, then single track on the old bridge and later on the new one. The new bridge was built on top of the existing structure and rested on the same piers. When the new one was completed, the old bridge was dismantled. The opening ceremony was carried out on 14th May 1914 by Lady Darnley.

During the First World War it was inevitable that the dockyard and various military establishments should increase in importance with the result that a considerable strain was put upon the tramway company. It was not long before, as with other systems, spare parts became scarce and there were staff shortages. Eventually one-third of the fleet was laid up in the depot, awaiting repair. As men were conscripted, women conductors were employed and, according to *The Times* of 4th June 1917, two local curates were among the part-time drivers taken on. There was some relief when the Sheerness system closed in 1917 since the company was able to acquire some second-hand equipment. Despite the various problems, the war years proved profitable with the heavy traffic ensuring increased receipts.

After the war it was some months before the system got back to normal but times were changing. Costs had risen, wages had increased and from the early 1920s competition from motor bus services increased. The end came nearer when in 1927 the British Thomson-Houston organisation sold their tramway involvement to the Maidstone & District Motor Services Ltd. Despite this, new management set about improving the tram's image by repainting all the cars – this time a simpler livery of unlined green and ivory. In 1928 car no 52 (the last to be purchased) was acquired second-hand from Maidstone

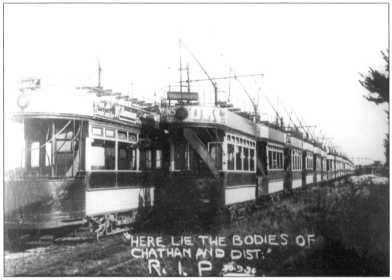

A sad sight – Chatham trams photographed on 30th September 1930. Abandoned tramcars left on the Rainham reserved track awaiting demolition. (John H. Meredith collection)

Corporation where trams were being replaced by trolleybuses. It was another United Electric car and, unlike Chatham's existing cars, was fitted with red carpet material along its long saloon seats.

Despite these improvements, closure of the tramway system was imminent. Trams had given the area sterling service for some 28 years but the new motor buses could offer a far more flexible service. In 1929 a Bill was passed enabling the Chatham company to run motor buses and change its name to 'Chatham & District Traction Co'. In October of that year an Order was obtained permitting replacement of all the company's trams and at the same time 37 Leyland 'Titan' double-deck buses were ordered. In addition work was put in hand to convert the Luton

Part of a tramcar body that escaped demolition. This inner saloon of Chatham car no 52 was photographed at Abbey Court Farm, at Lidsing, Chatham on 8th August 1953. (John H. Meredith collection)

depot for use by motor vehicles. The last tram ran on 30th September 1930 after which all the cars were driven to the private tracks on Rainham Road to form a long and forlorn double line of cars awaiting sale or destruction.

Very little remains today to show where the trams existed. The Luton depot near the Hen and Chickens survived to become a Maidstone & District repair depot for their National Buses. Between Rainham Mark and Rainham sections of the old preserved track remained for many years as grassed areas with flowerbeds. Some of the original retaining walls also survived – many becoming ivy-covered. At the main gate to the former dockyard, it remained possible to identify where a siding was located although the track has long since gone. At Pembroke Gate, white stone slabs inserted into a retaining wall indicating various destinations were visible for many years. These were later repainted for the buses.

The last car to climb Chatham Hill was driven by Mr Watson, a very large man who weighed 22 stone. It is said that, during the whole of his service, he never once went on top deck of a tram since he was too big to squeeze through the narrow way at the top of the stairs!

5
Bridging the Medway

Maidstone Corporation Light Railways

Maidstone's car no 2 used on the High Street to Barming service. Electric trams began in Maidstone in 1904. (Colin Withey collection)

Near the top of the High Street in Maidstone a Russian cannon stands in the centre of the road. The gun was captured during the Crimean War and was presented to the town in 1858 by Lord Panmure. Further up the street nearer the present-day Stoneborough Centre stands the Queen's Monument, presented to the town in 1862 to commemorate Queen Victoria's Silver Jubilee. Close by, a tram shelter was built early last century and it was from this point that Maidstone's first electric tram service began.

The initial route was from the High Street to Barming and this began on 14th July 1904. An official opening

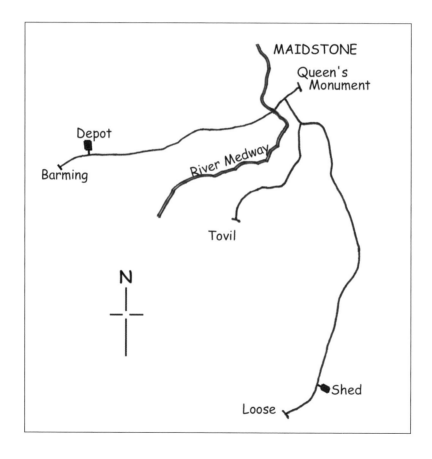

ceremony took place and four cars ran in procession along the route and afterwards a gathering of invited guests took place at the Town Hall. When a public service began soon afterwards, there were trams at 10 minute intervals throughout the day.

First ideas for a tramway in Maidstone came in 1880 when a private company put forward proposals for a horse tramway covering some seven routes including tracks to Barming, Tovil church and the Wheatsheaf along Tovil Road. The scheme seemed over ambitious for a town of sparse population at the time (less than 30,000) and there was considerable local opposition. Even so, Parliamentary Plans were deposited in 1881 but the Bill was withdrawn and nothing further was heard.

In 1900 consideration was given to electric tramways covering similar routes but extending to the Fountain

Maidstone trams pass at a loop near the Cherry Tree at Barming on the Tonbridge Road. (Lens of Sutton)

Inn at Barming, the Rose at Tovil and the King's Arms at Loose. In addition there were plans to reach the Running Horse at Sandling, Penenden Heath and the Ashford Road railway bridge but these lines did not materialise at any time. The proposals were again thought over-lavish and, in any event, were not approved in time for an Order in the next Parliamentary session.

In the end it was an application to the Light Railway Commissioners in May 1902 that finally got Maidstone its trams when permission was granted for a line from the top of the High Street to Barming. A track of 4 ft 8½

An aerial view of Maidstone's Barming depot. Today the site is occupied by flats although short sections of the original tram track can still be seen in the adjacent car park. (Lens of Sutton)

74

in gauge was proposed with a terminus at the Bull Inn but since this was outside the borough boundary, the line was agreed only to the Fountain Inn. In addition the permitted gauge was reduced to 3 ft 6 ins.

At about the same time, a company called the 'Rochester, Chatham, Gravesend & Maidstone Tramways Co' (the RCG&MT) was submitting a Bill for Parliament's 1903 session seeking powers to include a route from Gravesend to Maidstone. Since Chatham was included in the company's proposals, Maidstone Corporation was displeased and countered with its own plans to extend and also include a line to Maidstone. Faced with such strong opposition the RCG&MT withdrew.

According to volume 1 of the book *The Tramways of Kent* edited by G.E. Baddeley, the contract to build Maidstone's tramways went to Dick, Kerr & Co of Preston at a cost of £18,000. An overhead wire system was used and these were supported by poles from both sides of the road. Six open-top four-wheel cars were provided, manufactured by the Electric Railway and Tramway Carriage Works Ltd also of Preston and numbered 1 to 6. The cars carried 22 passengers inside and 26 on top and each was equipped with two Dick, Kerr 25B motors of 25 hp each. In the saloon, benches ran the length of the car covered with red carpet and there were maroon curtains at the windows.

The trams proved an immediate success and an extra car had to be ordered before the end of the year. The manufacturer was asked to produce a vehicle within seven weeks. The demand was speedily dealt with and delivery of car no 7 was made in February 1905. In the

Maidstone's car no 3 passes St Michael's church on Tonbridge Road bound for Barming. Note the lady on the top deck with her parasol open! (Colin Withey collection)

same year a parcels service began, with receiving offices opening at the terminals and in many local shops. Although the offices were subsequently abolished, the service continued to exist until 1969.

There is a story that the 15th-century half-timbered Wool House at Loose was once used by Cromwellian forces as a headquarters during the Civil War and there was also a time when it served as a fleece store for the local water-powered woollen mills. Nearby Tovil was once a village in its own right with paper mills giving the local folk their livelihood. Work began on lines to these outlying areas in 1907. The Tovil route was to serve the many terraced houses in King Edward's Road near the terminus at the Rose public house. Trams to Loose were

Car no 17 awaits return to Maidstone SER station (now Maidstone West) from the Loose tram terminus. Note the sapling planted to the left of the signpost and trolley pole. (Lens of Sutton)

A tram awaits departure at Maidstone's High Street terminus by the Queen's Monument. (Lens of Sutton)

routed along Loose Road and then down part of Old Loose Hill as far as the King's Arms. The Loose trams began in October 1907 mostly as single track with loops at a time when Loose Road was no more than a country lane. The Tovil service began in January 1908, also single track with loops, but the last stretch down Tovil Hill was double. Initially both routes started from the Queen's Monument but later they ran from further down the High Street, at the cannon.

To meet increased demand, a further ten tramcars were delivered during 1907 from The United Electric Car Co of Preston which had taken over the previous manufacturer. These were numbered 8 to 17 and were

Trams to Tovil began in 1908 but the traffic was disappointing. Within a year single-deck cars were used, one of the first pay-as-you-enter cars in service anywhere in Europe. (Lens of Sutton)

78

smaller in body than the previous cars, carrying 18 passengers inside and 22 outside. Other changes included folding platform steps and, instead of the earlier mechanical bell signals, electric bells were installed.

There was little further expenditure for a while since the Corporation had incurred heavy loans to meet existing work. In 1910 consideration was given to running Maidstone's trams to Chatham and also a route along Sutton Road to Sutton Valence was proposed. Neither of these happened but pressure remained for a service to the Penenden Heath area. This also did not come about, largely because two years earlier, the Commercial Motor Company, predecessor of the Maidstone & District Motor Services Ltd, had run

Maidstone High Street c. 1906. Trams lasted until 1930 when trolleybuses took over. (Lens of Sutton)

experimental services along Boxley Road and had found insufficient demand.

Traffic on the Tovil route proved disappointing and economies had to be effected. Soon a one-man single-deck 'demi-car' (no 18) was ordered and delivered from the United Electric Car Co in 1909. This was one of the first pay-as-you-enter cars in service anywhere in Europe and was used during peak periods only on the Tovil line, leaving it free to work the Loose route at other times. In 1913 there were again suggestions to provide a service on the Boxley Road route to Penenden Heath, this time by double-deck petrol-electric buses, but once again the idea was dropped because of 'losses anticipated'.

During the First World War, with most of the men called up into the forces, like other systems their places

A view of Maidstone, c1910, looking into the town from the bridge. The last tram to run in Maidstone was on the evening of 11th February 1930. Trolleybuses began the next day. (Lens of Sutton)

were taken by women. As expected during hostilities there were cuts in services but, despite inevitable lack of maintenance, the track and cars remained in pretty good condition. As the men returned after the war, so their places were refilled and the last woman left around the end of 1920.

In 1919 traffic had picked up on the Tovil route due to increase of business and double-deck trams were reintroduced. The new lease of life was, however, short-lived and soon thoughts of regular motor bus and trolleybus services were being considered. Early in 1923 the General Manager and the Chairman of the Transport

Three preserved vehicles can be found at Carleton Colville, the East Anglia Tramway Museum. Photographed August 2004, they are London Transport car 1858, Blackpool car 159 and Maidstone trolleybus 52. (John H. Meredith collection)

Committee visited Birmingham to inspect the new trolleybuses running there. But despite this, motor buses initially won the day and trolleybuses were not to follow until 1928, then at first only on the Queen's Monument to Barming route.

In 1924 the residents of Penenden Heath finally got their transport with a service of three single-deck Tilling Stevens petrol-electric vehicles from London Road along Boxley Road. Other routes followed and later two 'Express' buses were introduced, though not of the petrol-electric design. Finally at a council meeting in February 1924, it was formally decided that when tram routes came up for renewal, the trams should be replaced by trolleybuses. By May 1927 a tender for eight double-deck six-wheeled trolleybuses was accepted and at the same time work began to convert the Barming route.

The last tramcar ran on the evening of 11th February 1930, believed to be no 2. It left the cannon at 10.50 pm and ran to Loose where it reversed and travelled to the Wheatsheaf where a specially constructed siding had been prepared. The journey in an undecorated car was under the control of Mr King and the Mayor and Corporation were on board. The driver was Mr F. Rose who had commenced his employment in 1904 after having been employed by the contractors, Dick, Kerr & Co, on the construction of the Barming line.

The last tram joined others in the siding to await the breaker. As soon as the journey had been completed, all redundant wiring was cut down using a horse-drawn tower wagon, ready for trolleybus operation the next day.

There is a small reminder of Maidstone's former trams in Barming. For many years the tram depot site opposite the Cherry Tree public house was occupied by Tovil Coachworks Ltd. The building has since been demolished and replaced by a block of flats but short sections of the original tram track can still be seen in the adjacent car park. There was a hope that a Maidstone demi-car might have been preserved but time and the elements took their toll. Until several years ago, Dover Transport Museum had the remains of a demi-car but it was in a very bad condition. When the museum moved in January 2004 to its current site, the remains were considered too fragile to move but the attempt was made nevertheless. Unhappily, the weather had the last say when a gale blew it over. Then, as if to make sure, local youths made a bonfire of it!

6
Over the White Cliffs

Dover Corporation Tramways

Dover's car no 10 enters Buckland depot. Dover was the first town in southern England to have an electric tram system. They began in 1897. (Colin Withey collection)

The first serious attempt to introduce a tramway system in Dover was made on 9th November 1895 when a special meeting of the Dover Town Council voted by 19 to 2 in favour of introducing passenger transport to the town. Previously local travel had been provided by a

84

One of Dover's original trams passes the post office and Bench Street. Dover was the first town in the south to introduce electric trams. (Lens of Sutton)

number of privately-owned horse buses and the council considered that an improved overall service was becoming a necessity.

By July 1896 a provisional order had been made and confirmed by the Board of Trade and various modes of traction were under consideration. Gas-driven trams were fully investigated but it was decided to adopt electric traction. Tenders were invited and that of Dick, Kerr & Co was accepted for the supply of electrical equipment and rails. J.J. Briggs & Co of Blackburn was appointed to construct the permanent way.

Work commenced early in 1897 and on 27th April strong complaints were received from the residents of Strond Street who claimed that their road had been closed for 5 weeks for the laying of track. On 27th August there was a Board of Trade inspection of the line between Buckland Bridge and the Harbour station and trial trips commenced the following month in order that drivers might gain some experience.

On 6th September 1897 Dover became the first town in the south of England to introduce electric trams. A gauge of 3 ft 6 ins had been agreed, together with an overhead-

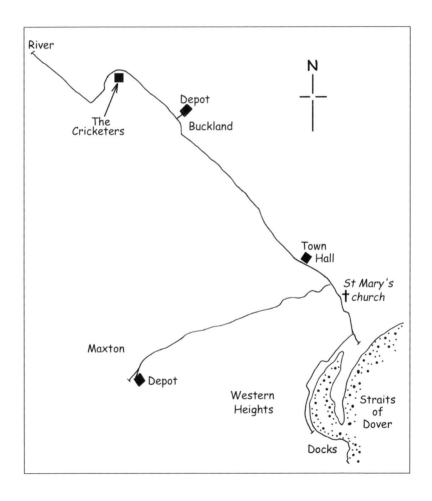

wire system. The trams earned immediate recognition from the *Railway World* which proclaimed, 'Leeds first, Dover second, the rest nowhere.' The periodical added, 'Why should London wait? Let them ask Dover Council for advice.'

Dover's first trams were built by Brush Electrical Engineering Co Ltd at Loughborough in 1897. Ten cars were delivered although when they arrived they had to be assembled in a field since the nearby depot at Buckland had not yet been completed. Cars had seating for 20 inside and 24 outside. Two had been supplied as trailers without electrical equipment although they were motorised within a year. Each vehicle was powered by two 25 hp motors and braking was by hand and rheostat.

The rheostat braking was of an early type requiring the controller handle to be brought back to the 'off' position and a key moved to a special 'braking' position before braking notches could be applied. It was a complicated arrangement, which, it was subsequently learned, a driver might be incapable of handling when in a situation of crisis.

The initial cars were four-wheeled and open-topped with platforms exposed to all weathers. On top the seating comprised transverse weatherproof 'flap' seats, thus ensuring that passengers in wet weather could sometimes find a dry seat! The trolley standard was to one side to conform with the position of the trolley wires and poles. The saloon seats were longitudinal and upholstered in red velvet but the material was soon to wear out and a type of carpet material was tried. Even this proved unsatisfactory and eventually slatted seats with no upholstery at all were fitted. The woodwork was of dark mahogany, which many considered gave the interior a gloomy effect further aggravated by a low-pitched roof.

The first vehicle, tramcar no 3, was ceremoniously driven by the Mayor, Alderman Henry Minter Baker, from the Town Hall up to Buckland, down to the Harbour station and then back to the Town Hall. Surprisingly there were no other celebrations. For the rest of the day a single car carried passengers and by the following day three cars were available providing a 15 minute interval service. Apparently this was the best that could be done since insufficient drivers had yet been trained.

The trams soon proved very popular. The public benefited immediately since fares were set at 1d all the way whereas horse bus charges from Buckland to the pier had been 4d. Initially the route-mileage was just over 3 miles and the total cost of the system had amounted to £28,000, which was considered a large sum for a small borough in such times. Yet the trams' success was reflected in the number of passengers over the first year, which amounted to 1,794,905. The Corporation made a net profit of £1,300 – the equivalent of a 1½d rate.

The second line to open was along Folkestone Road to Maxton. This was inspected on 10th December 1897 and opened a short time afterwards. A depot was built at Maxton next to the Orange Tree public house. At about the same time difficulty was being experienced with a section at Clarence Pier where trams were frequently delayed by a much-used railway level crossing. This stretch was abandoned in April 1898 with the result that tram services improved, with cars no longer delayed by closed crossing gates.

Car no 15 in Dover's Market Square. The car was built by J.G. Brill & Co of Philadelphia, USA. (Colin Withey collection)

In the middle of 1898 two more cars were acquired (nos 11 and 12) and two more (13 and 14) followed a few months later. This meant that a 5 minute service could now be provided on the main route to Buckland and a 10 minute service along Folkestone Road. In 1899 two more cars were delivered, having been built by J.G. Brill & Co of Philadelphia, USA.

Over the years there had been numerous proposals to link coastal towns throughout Kent. Another such idea surfaced in November 1899 when a private individual suggested a 'light railway of tramway type' between Ramsgate and Hastings. This was to connect with the Thanet Electric Tramways & Lighting Co's trams (soon to be opened), linking southwards to Dover's trams at the Market Square and then beyond Dover's tram-tracks at Maxton and on to Folkestone and Hastings. A single track with loops was being considered with current taken from overhead wires. Dover Corporation strongly opposed the scheme, feeling it would interfere with its own system, and the proposals, which gained little support elsewhere, were soon dropped.

Otherwise the year 1899 was relatively uneventful. Perhaps the most outstanding happening locally was when a newly-married couple hired a tram on 16th October of that year. The bridegroom was a member of the staff, Mr William Sinclair, and the bride was Miss Catherine Fakely of Buckland Farm House. A tram bedecked with white ribbons took the couple and their guests from Salem church to a reception at Buckland causing great interest and excitement among onlookers during the journey.

Local Sunday Schools frequently hired numbers of trams to take children out to Buckland for their annual treats. At the end of the day the trams made their way back through the main streets with the children cheering and singing along the route and the drivers often joining in with the clanging of their bells.

The trams generally were regarded as 'friendly' by the local folk who soon found the service cheap and reliable. Nobody was ever left behind because he or she was a few yards away from a stop and often a driver would give a friendly clang, clang on the bell to spur on an intending passenger. Until the end of the First World War there were only a few fixed stopping places and usually a car would pull up anywhere when needed. Fixed stops were first introduced as an economy measure.

During the tramway's early life, services were provided only on weekdays. After a number of years there was agitation for trams to run on Sundays. Long discussions followed at meetings of the Tramways Committee and the Town Council and in the end the idea was put to a vote. Sunday trams were defeated by a small majority and it was not until 1911 that the ban was relaxed.

Among proposals to extend were two schemes, one to reach River church and then on to Kearsney Abbey and the Alkham Valley and another to build a line from Dover seafront, up East Cliff to St Margaret's. After an enquiry in 1902, both ideas received permission but the River line was to terminate at Minnis Lane. Both schemes had been submitted by private companies but neither proceeded as had been intended. In 1904, however, the River extension interested the Corporation, which, in order to relieve acute local unemployment at that time, undertook its construction. The St Margaret's scheme was not pursued.

A £10,353 tender was accepted to build the River extension and in February 1905 work began. Even then there was much criticism as the contractors brought in a good deal of outside labour instead of using the local unemployed for whose benefit the work had been largely undertaken. When the new track opened in October 1905 the fare from River to the pier was fixed at 2d. Four new cars were purchased at £575 each to work the new tracks. Since the River service involved steep gradients, the braking included hand, rheostat and Spencer track brakes. The Spencer brakes were actuated by a large brass wheel concentric with the hand-brake staff.

At the junction of Elm Vale Road and Folkestone Road there is a shelter built during the 1920s for people using the Maxwell trams. (Author)

Despite such precautions, a serious accident occurred to car no 20 when it got out of control at the top of Crabble Hill on the River route. The car ran away down a 1 in 10 gradient in Crabble Road to overturn at the bottom, killing 11 passengers and injuring 60. The driver, who managed to jump off shaken but unhurt, stated at an inquiry that the brakes were useless and the emergency brake handle had jammed. Subsequent examination indicated that the rheostat brake had not worked because the driver had not switched off the power and had actually driven the car down the hill at full speed! The findings were that the accident was due to an error of judgment of an 'insufficiently experienced driver'. It was also pointed out that the consequences were much worse than they need have been owing to the serious overloading of the car. As a result, the carrying of passengers on the top deck was forbidden on this part of the line for the time being. It transpired that the driver had been discharged from the army as unfit after a nervous breakdown.

The River line was never considered to be a great success. By the end of the First World War, members of the Town Council were convinced they had chosen the wrong route because there had been little development along the line taken by the trams. Various plans to overcome this were considered but due to the high costs involved nothing was done.

During the 1914–18 war there was an acute shortage of spare parts as well as manpower. Later, as in other systems, women conductors were employed and even three women drivers were taken on. A rise in running costs was inevitable and as a result fares were increased.

A tram reaches Dover's northern-most terminus at River, photographed c1931. (W.E. Crawford/John H. Meredith collection)

The River service dwindled to one car an hour and some of the worn sections of track were lifted.

The first serious suggestions that the system should be abolished came soon after the war. The trams and tracks were run down and it was considered that some of the early profits should have been saved to meet renewal costs. A specialist produced a report condemning the entire system. It was recorded that even the overhead wires had worn so thin that they were considered dangerous. Rather than face such costs, the council looked for alternative solutions and in 1922 they attended a demonstration of a trolleybus (a primitive single-decker) but this did not prove encouraging. Meantime the local Trades Council, whose members found the trams convenient and cheap for getting to and from work, were leading a town campaign to 'reprieve'

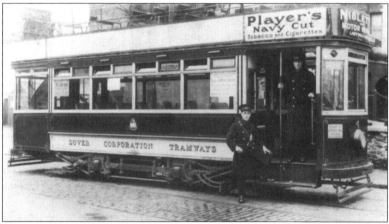

In 1927 Dover Corporation purchased 5 tramcars second-hand from West Hartlepool Corporation. Staff pose in this picture of car no 4. (Lens of Sutton)

the trams. In 1923 there were further plans to introduce trolleybuses but there was fierce opposition and nothing more was heard for some time.

Dover got its first covered-top trams in 1926 when cars 8 and 9 were delivered from Darlington. Five further cars followed in 1927 but these were open-top and purchased second-hand from West Hartlepool. More cars followed in 1930 when five were purchased from the Birmingham & Midland Joint Tramways Committee with four more from the Birmingham Corporation Tramways in 1933.

Despite replacements and track repairs, it was becoming clear the end was near. In April 1934 the East Kent Road Car Co offered to assist by providing services within the Borough. The council could not reach a decision so they called in an advisor who, within a short

Cars 25 and 26 fitted with top covers were purchased from the Birmingham & Midland Joint Tramways Committee in 1930. (Colin Withey collection)

time, was empowered to negotiate with the East Kent company. It was eventually agreed that buses would replace the trams and that the Corporation would receive three-quarters of the net profits.

Dover's trams came to an end on the night of 31st December 1936. Car no 10 (an ex Birmingham & Midland vehicle) ran as a ceremonial last car to arrive at the Maxton shed at 11.30 pm. The car was driven by the Mayor, Alderman G. Norman, and large 'L' plates had been fitted at the controls! As the first bus, no 97, took the Mayor and other dignitaries back to the Town Hall, the takeover by the East Kent company had been completed.

The now-redundant open-top tramcars were driven under their own power to a section of track on sleepers on the River extension to be destroyed by fire. The other cars were scrapped by contract. Forty years of loyal service by Dover's trams had come to an end.

Today some relics of the past remain. Both depots still exist – the Buckland Depot is now Hollis Motors where vague signs of former tram tracks can be found in the parts department. The old Maxton Depot next to the Orange Tree public house has been demolished to become a block of flats. At the junction of Elms Vale Road and Folkestone Road there is still a shelter built during the 1920s where people waited for the Maxton trams.

Until the 1960s two Dover tram bodies had survived the years. One was in use as a shed on a smallholding at Whitfield, near Dover, and another as a stable in a garden behind the Plough Inn between Folkestone and Dover. Unhappily both no longer exist. Also until a few years ago lengths of track existed forming the kerb on both sides of Green Lane Hill but following road

Dover's Buckland Depot is now Hollis Motors where indications of former tram tracks can be found in the parts department. (Photo courtesy of Hollis Motors, Dover)

widening, these must be presumed buried on site.

Dover Transport Museum in Willingdon Road, White Cliffs Business Park at Whitfield, is well worth a visit. Here numerous relics from the tram days can be seen. The museum is open on Wednesdays, Fridays and Sundays as well as bank holidays from Easter to the end of September. Although a complete tram cannot be seen, a fine 32 ft layout can be found with four Dover trams and one Maidstone tram in $\frac{1}{16}$th scale.

A book by Doug Welby called *The Kentish Village of River* includes an anonymous recollection of the early days of trams:

> 'If you've got a sluggish liver,
> Take a penny trip to River,
> On a tram.'

7
The Thanet Resorts

Thanet Electric Tramways & Lighting Co Ltd

Margate's car no 12 leaves The Fort, Cliftonville, bound for Ramsgate. When trams first came to the Isle of Thanet in 1901, they were crowded beyond capacity, often with passengers standing on the top deck. (Colin Withey collection)

In 1871 there was an ambitious proposal to build a tramway over 21 miles long, with a 4 ft 8½ in gauge, from Dover to the SER Ramsgate Town station. The idea came from the Dover, Deal, Sandwich and Ramsgate Tramway Company but it was refused. In its enthusiasm the company had assumed it would have the support of the

Turnpike Trustees but this did not prove correct so the Board of Trade disapproved.

A year later there was an even more ambitious plan covering nearly 30 miles of route, again starting in Dover, but this time following the coastal route to reach the Margate seafront at the Shakespeare public house. Royal Assent was given but the idea foundered through lack of finance. Further speculative proposals followed with plans to reach Hastings or even Brighton but it was eventually plans confined to the Isle of Thanet itself that had more success.

A proposal for a 2 ft 6½ in gauge horse tramway from Ramsgate to Margate via St Peter's was approved in 1879 and the following year the company was granted powers to use steam traction. In 1882 it was agreed the gauge should be widened to 3 ft 6 ins and a mile of track was actually completed from St Peter's church to Broadstairs railway station. The line received much opposition from Margate and Ramsgate councils and it was never completed. One of the reasons for disapproval was given in *Keble's Gazette* – this quoted a Margate councillor as complaining that with the proposed distance between the kerb and the tram lines being only a few inches in places, it would not leave adequate room for the ladies to pass in their fashionable dresses, which trailed about two feet behind them!

Other ideas came and went and it was not until the Light Railways Act was passed in August 1896 that progress was made. Although the Act was basically for railways, it was possible for a tramway that joined two or more authorities to take advantage of it. The Isle of Thanet Light Railways (Electric) Company Ltd was promoted in November 1896 by Mr William Murphy, the son of a Bantry building contractor, who became involved in tramway construction in many parts of the country as well as in Dublin, Belfast and Cork. His company's initial intention was to run 3 ft 6 in gauge electric trams from Pegwell Bay to Westgate via Ramsgate and Margate. Following an enquiry held at Ramsgate, the line to Pegwell Bay was dropped and, when an Order was submitted for approval by the Light Railway Commissioners, the section from Margate to Westgate was also omitted.

As a result, the Commissioners approved in December 1897 a line from Westcliffe New Approach Road, Ramsgate, via the LCDR Harbour station then northwards through Broadstairs to terminate at Westbrook, west of Margate. The Board of Trade's approval followed in August 1898 for a route of nearly nine miles to be built at an estimated cost of £67,595.

It was not long before application was made to extend the proposed line. In November 1898 the company applied for a further Order covering an extension along Ramsgate's Grange Road to the SER Ramsgate Town railway station and a further extension westwards from Westbrook to Westgate to terminate in Minnis Road at Birchington. There were objections to the latter with the result that the application for a line to Westgate and Birchington was withdrawn. The route to Ramsgate Town station was approved and the company had to be content with approval of only a short stretch at the northern end to the Westgate boundary at Westbrook.

In May 1899 the company changed its name to Isle of Thanet Electric Tramways & Lighting Company Ltd

100

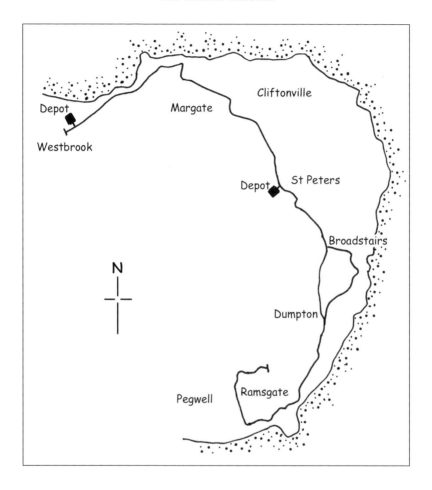

following approval to provide electric lighting in Margate and later in Broadstairs, a move that was to acquire much significance at a later date. In the same year Mr Murphy formed the Thanet Construction Company Ltd to build the tramway and the electric light systems at a cost of £450,000.

Work was soon in hand and 40 open-top and overhead-wire tramcars were ordered from the St Louis Car Co of America. All were fitted with two British Thomson-Houston (BTH) motors of 35 hp each. Cars 1 to 20 were four-wheeled vehicles whereas cars 21 to 40 were eight-wheeled with pony wheels towards the end of the car. Also cars 1 to 20 were fitted with four windows each side but the second batch comprised longer cars with six windows each side and a greater seating capacity. The livery until 1927 was rich maroon and yellowish cream.

A power station and car shed were built at St Peter's and a siding connected them with the LCDR railway line for the delivery of coal and other materials. The car shed, a large corrugated iron building, had a capacity for 40 cars with eight tracks. In 1902 a small depot was built at the Westbrook terminus. Current from the power station was supplied at 500 volts with batteries providing power and lighting during the night when the generators were not working.

The route commenced in Canterbury Road, Westbrook, which at that time was open country. After passing Margate Sands station on the seafront (closed in 1926) and then Margate West (today just Margate) the line passed close to the Dreamland Amusement Park (previously 'Hall by the Sea'). There was a time when Margate had as many as four different railway stations and if a planned LCDR terminus is included and another that was built but never used, the potential number increases to six! It was this last station that was never used that the railway authorities let to a firm of caterers who named it 'Hall by the Sea'. When it became part of the amusement park all traces of the railway were lost.

Eastwards from Margate the tramline continued to Northdown Road, the main street of Cliftonville. As buildings thinned out so the track entered private reservations and by Northdown Hill the line crossed open countryside. The St Peter's depot was situated where Northdown Hill joins Westover Road and about a mile beyond this, the lines separated. One route bypassed Broadstairs to be known as the 'Top Road' and the other, known as the 'Main Line' took trams along the High Street to reach the seafront along Victoria Parade. Tracks then continued along a private reservation to rejoin the 'Top Road' not far from Dumpton station. The 'Top Road' route took lines along Osborne Road and Salisbury Road and then entered a private reservation. Both these reservations became established roads in the 1960s long after the trams had gone – the 'Top Road' section became Salisbury Avenue and the 'Main Line' Dumpton Park Drive. The line concluded at the then Ramsgate Town station, having more or less circled the town.

Trial runs began in March 1901 mostly with car no 22 – a bogie car. Crowds collected along Madeira Walk and cheered when the tram derailed due to gauge inaccuracies. An official inspection took place later in the month after which the Board of Trade gave approval. The line opened for traffic on 4th April 1901 from Margate to Ramsgate Harbour via the 'Top Road'. Initially only eight cars could be used because sub-stations planned at each end of the line were not ready and power was inadequate.

It seemed that everybody on the Isle of Thanet wanted a ride. Cars were crowded beyond capacity with standing on the top deck, the stairs, inside and even on the buffers. The new conductors had great difficulty collecting fares. Everyone was pushing and nobody had the right money. It was evident that many rode without payment at all and some managed to travel all the way from Margate to Ramsgate for a penny ticket. In addition conductors sometimes had to help the drivers when trams left the rails! However, the trams were an instant success and over the subsequent Easter holiday over 9,000 fares were collected daily.

An obstacle to trams reaching Broadstairs was the need for a new railway bridge over the High Street but this was completed by early May and all the remaining portions of the route were opened on 6th July 1901. It was not long before a 'war' broke out. Inevitably flymen and brake proprietors were soon to lose business through competition and they did their best to obstruct the track. More than one cab was lost in a 'collision' during this time.

In a share offer made by the tramway company in the 11th December 1901 issue of *Electrical Investments*, reference was made to the profit earned during the first six months of running. This amounted to £13,610 despite the fact that the rolling stock was already proving inadequate. The offer referred to Ramsgate, Margate and Broadstairs as being 'the happy haunts of the cockney ... more crowded during the season than perhaps any other seaside resorts within easy reach of London.' It added that the tramways offered rides for several miles in sight of the sea, 'which meant more money to the company

104

A crowded tramcar rounds the corner at Ramsgate's Royal Parade, c. 1910. (Colin Withey collection)

than the mere intercommunication facilities (badly needed as they were) between the towns.'

The tramway company's future now appeared to be guaranteed and twenty more trams were ordered to meet demand. The first ten came from the British Thomson-Houston Company and, since more were needed as soon as possible, ten further cars came from a BTH order previously in hand for Chatham.

Despite such successes the tramway system found itself dogged with accidents throughout the next few years. In 1901 there were numerous minor incidents, enough to provoke a Board of Trade Inquiry, which was held on 15th June. The vicar of St Paul's church took advantage of the occasion to complain that the noise of trams on Sundays drowned his services but the Inquiry remained confined to accidents. Evidence indicated how there had been instances of broken axles, trolley arms leaving the wires and at one corner in Ethelbert Crescent, Cliftonville, nine cars had been derailed the previous week. The company countered by claiming the troubles had almost stopped and in ten weeks some 700,000 passengers had been carried with 140,000 miles covered.

Within two months a serious accident occurred. Car no 8 got out of control down Fort Hill, Margate, and overturned into shopfronts in King Street injuring 28 people. Staff car no 38 used jacks and chains to put the tram back on the track and it was driven back to the depot. Unfortunately car no 50, sent with equipment to clear up the mess, also got out of control and ran into the back of no 38, fortunately without injury. Track brakes were fitted to all four-wheel cars but it was found that the eight-wheeled cars with bogies presented problems. Special brakes were fitted but they were not successful. Eventually after two had collided, the drastic decision was made that either the bogie cars should be taken off the roads or their bodies shortened so that they could be remounted on standard single trucks. The latter course was followed but the work took many months and the cost was high.

There were further accidents in 1905. On 27th May car no 47 failed to take a bend in Ramsgate and ended up in a grocer's shop in Belle Vue Road. The driver and conductor were seriously hurt as well as the shopkeeper's seven year old daughter. The local council was concerned, commenting that 'people might think Ramsgate was quite a dangerous place to come to.'

Unhappily for the company, accidents continued. On 3rd August 1905 car no 41 got out of control in the rain

Trams pass along Margate's seafront on a warm day, c1910. In 1872 Royal Assent had been given for a plan to link Dover, Ramsgate and Margate with a route along the coast but this foundered through lack of finance. (Colin Withey collection)

down Ramsgate's Madeira Walk, ploughed through an iron fence and fell some 32 feet into ground at the rear of the Queen's Head public house. Fortunately just six passengers were on board and the only person seriously hurt was the driver. The *Daily Mirror* the next day described the situation quite dramatically stating, 'Amid the cries of the terrorised occupants, the huge car toppled over the edge and was hurled into space.'

The inquiry revealed that the driver had only nine days' experience as a motorman and had taken cars up and down Madeira Walk from the first day. Examination showed that the sanding gear had failed to operate and that the wheels had locked with the handbrake rendering the rheostat brake inoperative. It was decided to improve the track at this point and to ensure that in future only experienced drivers should be employed on the hills. Little wonder the trams acquired the nickname of 'yellow perils'.

The years that followed were more peaceful and the tramway company continued to show a steady profit. Development was mainly in the electric light business with new equipment installed and new sub-stations built. On 17th August 1912 a French aviator landed an aeroplane in a field opposite the power station and, to cope with capacity crowds, all 59 cars turned out. An onlooker commented that many trams had their life guards touching the ground because of the weight of the

A Ramsgate tram is temporarily delayed when a horse and cart blocks Madeira Walk. (Colin Withey collection)

crowds riding on them – but it was a great day.

The tramway company purchased three buses in 1913 and was at last able to serve Birchington, which had previously excluded trams as well as forbidding excursion trains. However, the buses brought in little extra revenue and they were probably second-hand vehicles.

During the First World War receipts fell and the area suffered badly from enemy attacks. During air raids, current was switched off and often trams were stranded in the rural areas although none was ever damaged. The first serious air raid came on 17th May 1915 when the Bull and George Hotel in Ramsgate's High Street was

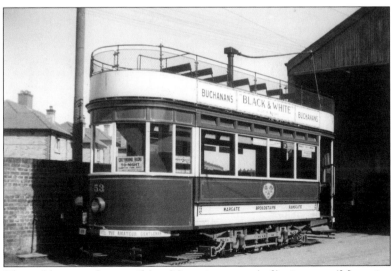

The side panel on this Margate car indicates a 'Margate–Broadstairs–Ramsgate' service. The board in the driver's compartment tells passengers 'Greyhound Racing tonight' and below the theatre announces a play 'The Amateur Gentleman'. (Colin Withey collection)

109

demolished with the loss of two lives. On 9th February 1916 there was a near miss when a bomb fell in the roadway close to a crowded tram near Montefiore College. The driver immediately pulled up, allowing the passengers to alight uninjured.

The tram depot itself narrowly escaped damage on the night of 20th May 1916 when a German Fokker aircraft – the first moonlight bomber over Thanet – dropped 15 bombs in the area. Apart from numerous broken windows, there was little damage except for a number of holes in the ground. According to a local press report, the only effective bomb was one dropped outside Peartree Cottage at Dumpton where one chicken was killed.

After the war the cars and the track were in poor condition. Only 14 cars were in good running order and others had been cannibalised to keep them going. Many were taken in for extensive repair or rebuilding. In 1924 the company obtained powers to supply electricity to Westgate and Birchington and changed its name to Isle of Thanet Electric Supply Company. It was apparent to many that electric supply had become the company's main interest. Generators were kept running overnight, a situation that benefited the night and early morning trams previously supplied from batteries. Competition from buses was becoming more intense with considerable rivalry from the East Kent Company although the tramway company was itself buying buses – used as feeders to the trams to avoid direct competition. In 1927 the tram's livery changed to a light crimson, and emerald green was chosen for the buses. It was thought that if the buses had also been red they would have been too similar to the East Kent buses.

The company's supply of electricity continued to give problems and when the price of current increased in January 1933, Margate Council irately considered that the electricity undertaking was subsidising the trams. A Transport Committee was formed to continually review the situation and in June 1935 the three local councils agreed to press the company to abandon the trams in favour of buses. The company eventually agreed to this in May 1936. At a stockholders' meeting in August of that year it was decided that the company's omnibus undertaking would also be sold to the East Kent Road Car Co Ltd, for £175,000.

The last car, no 20, made the final trip on the night of Wednesday, 27th March 1937 with the usual 'celebrations' plus a band. Earlier 'last cars' in each direction had been driven by the mayors of the towns through which they passed with the town clerks acting as conductors. Early next morning scarlet and cream East Kent Leyland 'Titan' buses commenced services. Motor buses and motor cars had won the day and 36 years of trams in Thanet were over.

A Dover contractor acquired the rails in return for removing them and, it is said, sold them to the Germans in time for them to make munitions for the Second World War! All the trams were demolished at the depot despite an effort to retain one for preservation.

8
A Pier Tramway and a Coastal Ride

Herne Bay Pier Tramway
The Hythe & Sandgate Tramway

Herne Bay Pier tramway came to an end during the Second World War. After the war a miniature railway was constructed, picture taken September 1948. The narrow-gauge track was built on the abandoned tram track. (John H. Meredith collection)

Herne Bay Pier Tramway

After its opening in June 1832, Herne Bay Pier became famous for its length, which at 3,640 ft, made it one of the longest in Europe. The narrow-gauge tramway, built to serve steamer traffic from London, was probably laid at the same time, being one of the first of its kind in the country. In the booklet *Pier Railways*, K. Turner writes that initially hand-propelled four-wheeled wagons were used to convey steamer passengers' luggage, although in June 1833 a sail-powered car was tried. Fitted with a lug sail for use when the wind was favourable, and hand-propelled when not, the vehicle was named 'Old Neptune's Car'. The idea had its problems and at least one death was recorded following an accident caused by the car's unexpectedly speedy progress.

However Herne Bay, then a mere village, did not at the time develop into the resort many had hoped. In addition harsh weather and wood-boring worms soon ended the life of the wooden pier. Closure came in 1864 but plans for a new iron structure were put in hand. Completed in 1873 it was only 320 ft long but an extension, retaining the tram track for public use, followed in 1898. It was now 3,920 ft long and among the longest in England.

Conversion to electric traction was completed the same year. The track gauge was between 3 ft and 3 ft 6 ins (records are not precise) and current at 250 volts DC was supplied through an off-centre conduit. Initially a Brush car was used driven by two 50 hp motors and in 1901 two trailers were purchased from the Bristol Tramways & Carriage Co where they had earlier served as horse trams. They were driven one at either end. A fourth vehicle purchased from Dick, Kerr & Co served as a luggage trolley.

Problems followed. There was a bad accident on 16th July 1901 when a trailer crashed into the sea. It happened when a luggage trolley at the front and running light left the track to jam itself against the railings. This caused the first car to crash through the railings and somersault down into the water. A rowing boat was used to pick up passengers and the car was recovered at low tide. One woman was killed in the incident. The pier was closed and a scheduled performance of 'The Jollity Boys' was abandoned. This hardly perturbed holidaymakers who, according to press reports, watched the ongoing spectacle from the beach anticipating the 'thrill' of additional bodies being discovered. Fortunately, they waited in vain.

In 1905 after financial losses the general manager was prosecuted for embezzlement and a receiver was appointed. In 1908 the pier was sold to the Herne Bay Urban District Council. The tramway survived until the First World War when the steamer trade ceased and the cars became temporary shelters on the pier. They were later sold for scrap.

When the steamers returned after the war the need arose again for a tramway. In July 1925 a petrol-electric tram was delivered but this proved unreliable. Eventually in 1934 a battery car that could seat 48 passengers was delivered (the old conduit had gone) and the earlier petrol-electric engine was adapted as a trailer. The battery car was a green and cream enclosed vehicle driven by an 11 hp Metrovick motor and its batteries were charged in a shed at the shore end of the single line. By 1939 traffic warranted a 15 minute service but this was not to last. War intervened once again, the trams ceased running and the pier was heavily fortified. The cars, which had given pleasure to so many, were sold for the pitiful sum of £12 10s as scrap.

A Strode petrol-electric tram at Herne Bay Pier on 14th February 1948. The gauge was 3 ft 4½ ins. (John H. Meredith collection)

The Hythe & Sandgate Tramway

Many Acts were submitted and either approved or rejected before a tramway from Hythe to Sandgate was constructed. At one stage tramlines of 3 ft 6 ins were proposed and at another a steam locomotive was purchased from the Sudan to work the lines but neither

An open toast-rack tram on the Hythe & Sandgate tramway stands outside St Paul's church. The tramway opened for traffic in May 1891. (Colin Withey collection)

idea was adopted. Finally standard gauge was agreed with horse traction only to be used. The South Eastern Railway (SER) contributed towards the capital cost.

The first tramline to be completed ran from Sandgate School to the Seabrook Hotel (later the Imperial Hotel) via Sandgate High Street, the Esplanade, the Promenade and Princes Parade. The section opened in May 1891 with the service operated by the Folkestone, Sandgate & Hythe Tramways Company. Folkestone was never reached, partly because of the steep hills involved and partly because of strong local objections.

Construction towards Hythe continued via South Road, Stade Street and Rampart Road, terminating in Red Lion Square and this was opened in June 1892. This

116

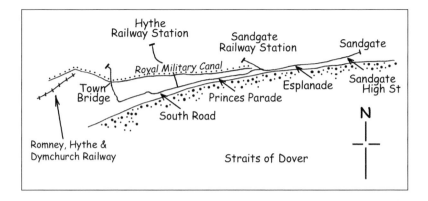

section contained many sharp curves and cars were equipped with water tanks on the platforms with taps which could be turned on to lubricate the wheels when bends were negotiated.

In 1893 the SER was authorised by Parliament to take on complete responsibility for the tramway at a cost of nearly £27,000. It was considered this might be part of a strategy by the SER to acquire a working site for a future Channel Tunnel project! After the takeover staff were fitted out with railway guard type uniforms. There were advantages with a railway involvement since at Sandgate there was a physical connection between tram and train lines. This was put to good advantage when any of the five tramcars available needed overhaul. The car was transferred to the railway and taken to Ashford Works for the necessary repairs.

When the war came in 1914 trams were suspended due to the shortage of horses, which were needed in France. Trams restarted in 1919 but horses were still difficult to find so ex-army mules were tried instead. The

In 1893 the South Eastern Railway took over the Hythe & Sandgate Tramway. The tramway lasted until September 1921. (Photograph courtesy of Folkestone Library)

A horse is about to be attached to Hythe & Sandgate tramcar no 1. During the First World War mules had to be used but they were erratic. They stopped in wrong places and often tried to walk into the wrong street! (John H. Meredith collection)

result apparently was catastrophic. The mules were erratic and not only stopped in the wrong places but often tried to walk in the wrong direction or into the wrong street. Horses were reinstated as soon as possible.

Already the tram service was beginning to lose its appeal. Uniforms were no longer provided and there were no winter services. When trams stopped for the season on 30th September 1921 it was to be for the last time. However, matters did not rest there. The council wrote to the SER (by then South Eastern & Chatham Railway) saying that the track would be replaced with

A standard gauge horse-drawn open 'tramcar' conveys passengers along the front between Hythe and Sandgate, c. 1918. (Pamlin Prints)

Kentish ragstone at the railway's expense. The railway reacted by stating they wished to exercise their option under the Tramways Act and carry out the work themselves. The council was not interested and told the railway company that any reinstatement would render them liable for costs plus surveyor's fees. The matter appeared to end there.

It is already more than 85 years since the horse tram days, which lasted almost 30 years. What a splendid tourist attraction such a system might be if it were to appear today.

Conclusion

The decline of the tram was as dramatic as its development. The first electric system to fail in Kent (in fact in the British Isles) was at Sheerness in 1917, a system that had been denied expansion by the railway. Twelve years later in 1929 Gravesend's tramways came to an end. The remainder of Kent's tramways all disappeared during the 1930s.

The majority had suffered during the First World War with lack of repairs and severe shortages of materials. At the same time many systems were more heavily used – often carrying workers to munitions factories. After the war their popularity increased for a time but the role of the motor vehicle in road transport was also increasing and the motor bus was becoming more reliable. At the same time the trolleybus, inheriting the ruggedness and the reliability of the tramcar, was growing in importance.

The tramway era lasted on average just over 30 years in Kent. During that time, the systems performed a very important function but towards the end they outlived their usefulness.

Trams failed for numerous reasons. Corrugation (uneven track wear) had always been a problem, with replacement a costly item. Track usually lasted about 15–20 years and often no allowance had been made for repair. Track brakes added to the wear on the track. A further serious weakness of the trams was the inability in some instances to provide through services because of competing tram companies. Only too quickly motor buses took advantage of such a situation.

The Tramways Act of 1870, although initially bringing about many road improvements at no cost to the local ratepayer, had proved a burden for the tramway companies. The Act had originated from the days of the horse trams when horses would wear out the road surface and, through the Act, tramway undertakings were committed to the cost of paving and repairing the roadway between the rails and 18 inches outside the track. This caused much aggravation in later years when motor traffic, including rival motor buses, was often responsible for the condition of the road. A further costly problem for tram companies was the assessment of their tracks at their full value for rating purposes.

On the Continent many countries have kept up with technology to provide trams in towns as well as on segregated tracks. In Britain since the 1950s the realisation has come that the wholesale removal of the tram from our cities has had financial, social and environmental disadvantages. The success of the Tyne & Wear Metro caused a flood of proposals to build new tramways in towns and cities throughout the UK. Within a year, the Tyne & Wear Metro was followed by the Docklands Light Railway, Manchester Metrolink, Sheffield Supertram, Midland Metro, Croydon Tramlink and many others.

In Kent no plans currently exist for the return of trams. A project is, however, under consideration called 'Fastrack' that will begin life as a guided busway. Although there was an aspiration amongst some that this would become a tram route in the longer term there are no plans at present and it is likely that it will remain a guided busway.

It is proposed the busway will eventually serve Dartford, Gravesend and Northcliffe. Its purpose is to meet the planned growth of development within the Kent Thameside area, coping with future transport demands and discouraging the use of unnecessary and excessive car use.

Today a visit to the Transport Museum at Covent Garden in London is necessary to see trams of the past, or perhaps further afield at the National Tramway Museum at Crich in Derbyshire where a tram ride can recall earlier times. As our towns become more and more congested, it is inevitable that many more alternative transport systems must come about. Failure to do so will surely lead to our town centres reaching an eventual complete traffic standstill.

Is it possible that trams in Kent will one day follow other parts of the UK and make a come-back?

Initial Opening and Closure Dates of Regular Electric Tram Services

Location	Opening Date	Final Closure
Dover	6 Sept 1897	31 Dec 1936
Isle of Thanet	4 Apr 1901	27 March 1937
Chatham	17 June 1902	30 Sept 1930
Gravesend	2 Aug 1902	28 Feb 1929
Sheerness	9 Apr 1903	7 July 1917
Bexleyheath	1 Oct 1903	23 Nov 1935
Maidstone	14 July 1904	11 Feb 1930
Erith	26 Aug 1905	9 Nov 1935
Dartford	14 Feb 1906	23 Nov 1935

Herne Bay Pier Tramway opened initially in June 1832 to serve steamer traffic from London. The tramway finally closed when war intervened in 1939.

The Hythe & Sandgate Tramway (horse-drawn) opened initially in May 1891 and the tramway finally closed on 30th September 1921.

The above does not include any experimental electrical systems, which did not provide a regular service to passengers.

Bibliography

Baddeley, G.E. (Ed), by 'Invicta' *The Tramways of Kent, Vols 1 & 2* (The Light Railway Transport League in association with The Tramway & Light Railway Society)

Baddeley, G.E. (Ed), by 'Southeastern' *The Tramways of Woolwich and South East London* (The Light Railway Transport League in association with The Tramway & Light Railway Society)

Bull, C.R. *The Tramways of Gravesend and Northfleet* (Kent County Library Local History Pamphlet, No 19)

Day, John R. *London's Trains and Trolleybuses* (London Transport)

Fayne, Eric *Tramways of the Medway Towns* (Trams October 1965)

Horn, J.V. *The Story of the Dover Corporation Tramways 1897–1936* (The Light Railway Transport League)

Kain, Daniel & Coates, Malcolm *The Trolleybuses of Maidstone* (The British Trolleybus Society)

Klapper, Charles *The Golden Age of Tramways* (Routledge & Kegan Paul)

Lee, Charles E. *The Hythe & Sandgate Tramway* (*Railway Magazine* October 1950)

Turner, K. *Pier Railways* (Oakwood Press)

Voice, David *London's Tramways* (Patrick Stephens Ltd)

Welby, D. *The Kentish Village of River* (Crabwell Publications)

Wilson, Geoffrey *London United Tramways 1894–1933* (George Allen & Unwin Ltd)

INDEX

Abbey Wood 23, 26, 29
Abbey Wood Depot 24

Balfour, Beatty & Co. Trams
  18
Barming 71 *seq*
Barnham Road Depot 12
Beer (Mr) 15
Bexley 9, 14, 23
Bexleyheath 15, 17 *seq*
Bexley Urban District
  Council Tramways 11–33
Birchington 109, 110
Birmingham & Midland
  Joint Tramways
  Committee 95, 96
Board of Trade 36, 59, 85, 99,
  105
Briggs (J.J. Briggs & Co) 85
Brill (J.G. Brill & Co) 89
British Electric Traction Co
  Ltd (BET) 38, 41, 48, 53
British Thomson-Houston
  Co Ltd (BTH) 60, 68, 102,
  105
British Westinghouse Ltd 24
Broadstairs 101 *seq*
Brooks (G.W.) 35
Brush Electrical Engineering
  Co Ltd 19, 24, 36, 40, 51,
  57, 66, 67, 87, 113
Buckland 86 *seq*

Burnham Road 17

Chatham & District Light
  Railways Co 56–70
Chatham & District Traction
  Co 69
Cheyney Rock 52, 54
City of Birmingham
  Tramways Co 53
Commercial Motor
  Company 79
County of Kent Electrical
  Power Distribution Co Ltd
  48
Crabble Hill 92
Cutbush (Mr) 49

Dartford 9, 13, 16 *seq*
Dartford Urban District
  Council Tramways 11–33
Dareneth Valley Hospital
  33
Darent Valley Tramway 15
Darlington Corporation 55
Deal 9
Demi-cars 25, 37, 40, 54, 80,
  83
Denton 37, 38, 43
Dick, Kerr and Co 13, 19, 31,
  38, 75, 82, 85
Doncaster Corporation
  Tramways 25